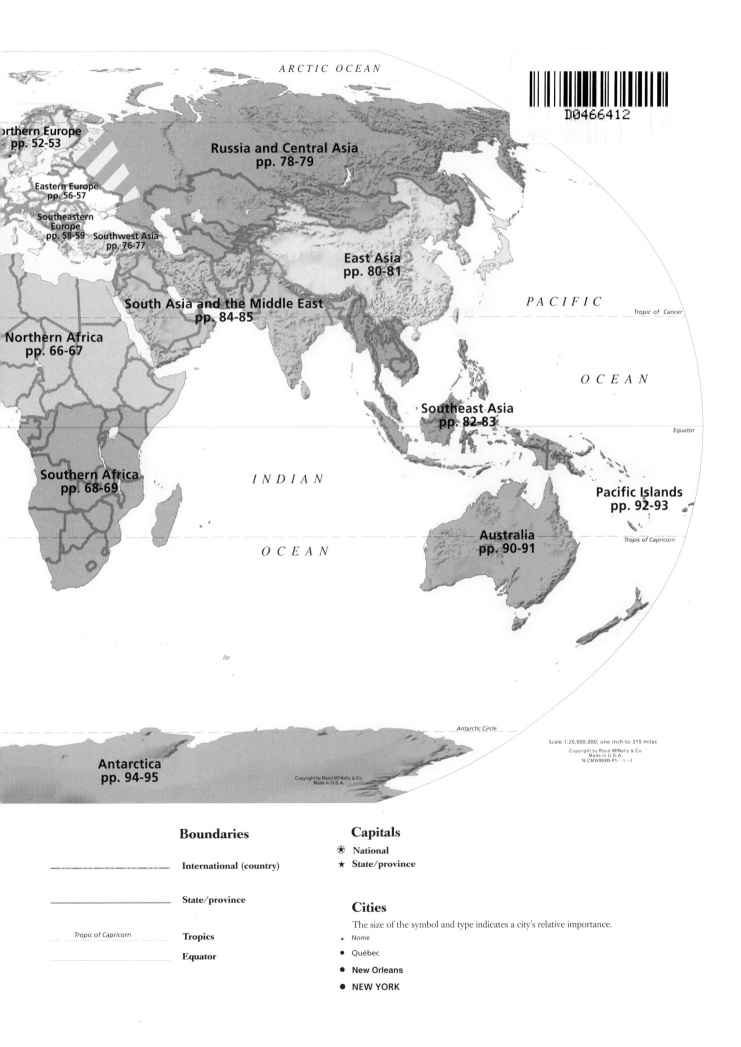

ARCTIC OCEAN

Northern Europe
pp. 52-53

Russia and Central Asia
pp. 78-79

Eastern Europe
pp. 56-57

Southeastern
Europe
pp. 58-59   Southwest Asia
pp. 76-77

East Asia
pp. 80-81

PACIFIC

South Asia and the Middle East
pp. 84-85

Tropic of Cancer

Northern Africa
pp. 66-67

OCEAN

Southeast Asia
pp. 82-83

Equator

Southern Africa
pp. 68-69

INDIAN

Pacific Islands
pp. 92-93

OCEAN

Australia
pp. 90-91

Tropic of Capricorn

Antarctic Circle

Scale 1:20,000,000; one inch to 315 miles

Antarctica
pp. 94-95

Boundaries

——— · ——— · ——— International (country)

——————— State/province

Tropic of Capricorn **Tropics**

Equator

Capitals

✹ **National**

★ **State/province**

Cities

The size of the symbol and type indicates a city's relative importance.

· Nome

● Québec

● **New Orleans**

● **NEW YORK**

**President and CEO,
Rand McNally & Company**
Richard J. Davis

**Senior Vice President,
Marketing**
Margaret A. Stender

**Director, Reference and
Children's Publishing**
Kendra Ensor

Editors
Brett Gover
Chris Jaeggi
Bobby Mort
Ann Natunewicz
Nathalie Strassheim

Art Direction and Design
John Nelson
Donna McGrath

Writers
Leslie Morrison
Catherine VanPatten

Marketing
Leslie Hoadley
Alexsandra Sukhoy

Photo Research
Feldman & Associates, Inc.

Manufacturing
Terry D. Rieger

Cartography
Robert K. Argersinger
Gregory P. Babiak
Barbara Benstead-Strassheim
Marzee Eckhoff
Winifred V. Farbman
Robert Ferry
Amy Sayers
Nathan Schroeder
David Simmons
Jill M. Stift
Thomas Vitacco

⊛ RAND McNALLY

Children's Millennium® Atlas of the World
Copyright © 2000 by Rand McNally & Company

`randmcnally.com`   `randmcnallykids.com`

Published and printed in the United States of America

"Millennium" is a registered trademark of Rand McNally & Company
Rand McNally and Company.
　　Children's millennium atlas of the World/Rand McNally.
　　p. ; cm.
　　At head of title: Rand McNally.
　　Includes index.
　　SUMMARY: Maps, photographs, illustrations, and text present information about the countries of the world, arranged by continents.
　　ISBN 0-528-84205-6 (hardcover)
　　ISBN 0-528-84207-2 (pbk.)
United States--Maps for children. 2. Children's atlases.
　　1. Children's Atlases [1.Atlases. 2. Geography.] I. Title. II.
Title: Rand McNally children's millennium atlas of the world
　　G1021 .R1647 1999 <G&M>
　　912--dc21

99-16119
CIP
MAPS

For information on licensing and copyright permissions, please contact us at
licensing@randmcnally.com

10 9 8 7 6 5 4 3 2 1

Photo Credits

(l = left, c = center, r = right, t = top, b = bottom)

© Mary Altier, 72 (b l)

Animals Animals:
© Dani/Jeske, 68 (b c)

Peter Arnold, Inc.:
© Fred Bavendam, 92 (b c); © Kevin Schafer, 46 (t); © Still Pictures/Mark Edwards, 16 (c l), 49 (t r); © Fritz Polking, 7 (t r), 68 (t l); © Bruno P. Zehnder, 90 (b r)

Black Star:
© F. Charton, 74 (b l)

© Cameramann International, Ltd., 80 (b c)

Bruce Coleman, Inc.:
© Andris Apse, 89 (c l); © Bruce Stewart, 88 (c l)

© Corbis/ *.Heaton*: 64 (b l)

Leo DeWyes, Inc.:
© DeWyes/D&J Heaton, 60 (t)

© European Space Agency, 6 (c)

FPG:
© Walter Bibikow, 31 (c r); © John Giustina, 15 (t r), 37 (b r), 81 (c r), 94-95 (b); © Mark Green, 26 (c l); © Peter Gridley, 24 (b l); © Steve Hix, 59 (b r); © G. Marche, 76 (c r); © Richard Price, 26 (c r); © Gail Shumway, 35 (b c); © Telegraph Colour Library, 70 (t), 80 (t l), 94 (t); © VCG, 15 (b r)

First Image West:
© Jim P. Garrison, 33 (b r)

© David R. Frazier Photolibrary, 49 (b l)

© Robert Fried Photography, 54 (b l)

H. Armstrong Roberts:
© B. Pogue, 56 (b l); © M. Schneider, 58 (b c); © Smith/Zefa, 88 (c r)

© Dave G. Houser, 91 (c r)

© Randall Hyman, 56 (c l)

© Jason Laure':
63 (c l); 64 (t r & b c)

Liaison International:
© Rob Johns, 27 (b l)

(c) Buddy Mays/TravelStock:
54 (t l), 88 (b), 91 (t)

© North Wind Picture Archives: 8 (Leif Ericsson, corn, iron plough), 9 (cotton gin, Abraham Lincoln, James Cook)

Odyssey Productions:
© Robert Frerck, 83 (c r)

Panoramic Images:
© China Photo Library, 70 (b); © Philip Gray, 86-87 (b); © Allen Prier, 24-25 (b); © K. Yamashita, 46 (b)

© Chip & Rosa Marie Peterson, 40 (b), 44 (c l)

© PhotoDisc, 8 (teacup), 11 (b r), 13 (b r), 33 (t r), 46 (b l), 60 (b l), 63 (b), 76 (b)

PhotoEdit:
© David Young-Wolff, 28 (b l)

Photo Researchers, Inc.:
© Tom McHugh, 89 (b l)

Photri:
77 (c l & c), 79 (cotton), 85 (Bangladesh); © Richard T. Nowitz, 74 (Muslims); © Fritz Prenzel Photo, 90 (c l)

Reuters/Archive Photos: © Yannis Behrakis, 58 (t r)

© Eugene Schultz, 69 (b c)

© The Stock Market:
41 (b r); © David Ball, 6 (b l), 55 (c r); © Peter Beck, 27 (b r); © Tom Brakefield, 79 (b r); © Tibor Bognar, 85 (b r); © Alex Cabral, 43 (b r); © Murilo Dutra, 40 (c r); © Mark Ferri, 23 (b r), 50 (b l); © H.P. Merten, 53 (t r); © James Marshall, 43 (t c);

© M. Mastrorillo, 45 (b r); © J. Pollerross, 84 (b r); © Alan Reininger, 83 (t c); © Torleif Svensson, 83 (c), 85 (Indian man); © Ben Simmons, 49 (b r)

© Stock Montage, 10 (Atlas)

Tony Stone Images:
92 (c r), 95 (t r); © Jerry Alexander, 56 (b r); © Glen Allison, 33 (horse farm), 92 (t r); © Christopher Arnesen, 59 (t r); © Horst Baender, 31 (t r); © Alejandro Balaguer, 40 (c r); © James Balog, 28 (Inuit), 68 (b r); © David Barnes, 89 (c r); © John Beatty, 23 (t r); © Tom Bean, 34 (c l); © Oliver Benn, 28 (t r), 57 (t l); © Grilly Bernard, 66 (b l); © Randa Bishop, 39 (c r); © Gary Braasch, 14 (c l); © Ernest Braun, 21 (t r), 39 (b l); © Gary Brettnacher, 79 (b l); © Paula Bronstein, 59 (b l); © Bushnell/Soifer, 83 (t l); © Marc Chamberlain, 68 (c l); © Paul Chesley, 81 (b l), 82 (b l); © Connie Coleman, 6 (b r), 53 (b l); © Bruno De Hogues, 7 (t l), 64 (c l); © Nicholas DeVore, 53 (b c); © Florence Douyrou, 6 (b c), 50 (t l); © Wayne Eastep, 73 (t r); © Chad Ehlers, 92 (b l); © R. Elliot, 85 (t c); © Fred Felleman, 95 (b r); © Robert Frerck, 40 (t c); © Stephen Frink, 20 (b l), 89 (b r); © Louis Grandadam, 77 (b r); © Sylvain Grandadam, 7 (t r), 64 (b r), 84 (t l); © Bob Handelman, 28 (b l); © George Haling, 6 (c r), 44 (b r); © Elizabeth Harris, 6 (c l), 22 (b l), 40 (b r); © Mark Harris, 28 (playground); © Paul Harris, 7 (c r), 74 (t r); © Gary Hayes, 50 (c l); © William J. Hebert, 45 (c l); © David Hiser, 6 (c r), 33 (t l), 55 (t r); © Jeremy Horner, 9, 36 (t); © George Hunter, 83 (b r); © Warren Jacobs, 17 (t r), 63 (t r); © Jacques Jangoux, 43 (t l & t r); © Gavriel Jecan, 58 (c l), 59 (t l); © Darrell Jones, 16 (t l); © Richard Kavlin, 33 (surfers); © Paul Kenward, 44 (t l); © Jerry Kobalenko, 78 (b r); © John Lamb, 69 (b r); © Susan Lapides, 28 (waiters); © Jane Lewis, 84 (c l); © Mark Lewis, 35 (c r); © Renee Lynn, 64 (Masai); © Yves Marcoux, 30 (t c); © Sally Mayman, 66 (b r); © Steve Outram, 51 (b r); © Bryan Parsley, 21 (b r); © Richard Pasmore, 49 (c r); © Orion Press, 81 (t r); © Colin Pryor, 36-37 (b); © Kevin Schafer, 40 (t l), 79 (railway), 95 (c l); © Herb Schmitz, 76 (c l); © Ian Shaw, 56 (t r); © Hugh Sitton, 69 (t r); © Charles Sleicher, 34 (b r); © Philip & Karen Smith; 44 (b l); © Robin Smith, 90 (b l); © Sarah Stone, 35 (t r); © James Strachan, 66 (b c), 79 (t r); © Keren Su, 72 (t r); © T. Resource, 44 (t r); © Tom Till, 6 (c l), 17 (b r), 24 (t); © Traveler's Resource, 73 (b l); © P. Tweedie, 90 (t); © Marie Ueda, 7 (kangaroo); © Larry Ulrich, 32 (b l); © Steve Vidler, 57 (t r), 63 (c r); © Rosemary Weller, 63 (t c); © Randy Wells, 35 (b r); © Art Wolfe, 19 (t r), 55 (b r), 68 (b l)

© SuperStock:
6 (Galileo), 7 (c l & fan), 8 (Christopher Columbus, Normans, Medici, Gutenberg, Arab traders, Ming mask), 9 (Model T, Galileo, Isaac Newton), 18 (b l), 19 (b r), 28 (b r), 30 (c l, b l, and b c), 38 (t r), 39 (t r), 42 (b l), 48 (c l), 52 (b r), 64 (t l and c r), 70 (c l), 74 (c l , c, and monks), 75 (c r), 80 (b r), 81 (b r), 82 (c l), 86 (t); © Avid Northcott, 43 (c r)

Vandystadt/Allsport:
© Jean-Marc Loubat, 55 (b l)

Viesti:
© M. Downey, 75 (t r)

Visuals Unlimited:
© Bill Kamin, 58 (b r); © Steve McCutcheon, 9, 62 (t l)

© Randy Wells, 50 (b c)

RAND McNALLY
Children's
Millennium® Atlas
of the
World

Contents

Millennium Timeline (The Years 1000-2000 A.D.)

	1000-1100	1100-1200	1200-1300	1300-1400	1400-1500	
North America	**c. 1000** Leif Ericsson and the Vikings sail to North America. **c. 1100** Anasazi begin building Mesa Verde cliff dwelling in southwestern North America.	**1100-1200** Hohokam of Arizona begin to build platform temple mounds for worship.	**c. 1200** Thousands live in and around Cahokia, a city of temple mounds built by the Mississippians. **1275-1300** Severe drought in Chaco Canyon hastens collapse of Anasazi communities.	**1300s** Warrior knights help make Aztecs a powerful society in Mexico. **1325** Aztecs found city of Tenochtitlán, now Mexico City.	**1492** Christopher Columbus lands in the Caribbean, but thinks he is in the East Indies.	
South America	**c. 1000** Peruvian farmers grow potatoes and corn for food.	**1100s** Incas in Peru make sculptures of their warrior chiefs.	**c. 1250** Mayan culture becomes stronger, and a new capital city is built. **c. 1250** Chimu people along northern coast of Peru expand their empire.	**c.1300s** Inca people in Peru become skilled builders. Inca culture expands into the central Andes region.	**1400s** Inca empire covers most of the west coast of South America. **c. 1450** Incas build Machu Picchu in Peru. **1470s** Chimu culture in Northern Peru collapses.	
Europe	**c. 1050** Iron plows replace wooden plows in Europe. **1066** Norman conquest of England.	**1119** First European University established in Bologna, Italy. **1124-1153** David I rules Scotland. **1152-1190** Frederick I rules powerful Holy Roman Empire.	**1215** King John of England signs the Magna Carta, limiting royal power. **1233** Coal is mined in Newcastle, England, for the first time. **1298** English archers use longbows to defeat Scottish army.	**1378-1381** Workers' Revolt in Florence, Italy (1378) and Peasants' Revolt in England (1381). **1397** Medici family establish themselves as bankers in Florence.	**1440s** Nicolas Cusanus claims the Earth is in constant motion and that space is infinite. **c. 1450** Johannes Gutenberg invents the printing press.	
Africa	**1000s** Bantu-speaking people hunt and farm in Africa. **1000s** West African kingdoms flourish from gold trade in Africa.	**c. 1100** Empire of Ghana begins to decline. **c. 1100** Arab traders settle in Africa along Indian Ocean coast. **1173** Muslim warrior Saladin declares himself sultan of Egypt.	**1200s** The town of Great Zimbabwe is built by the Shona people in southern Africa. **1235** Mali empire in West Africa becomes more powerful.	**1348** The Black Plague devastates Egyptian population. **c. 1350** Great Zimbawe in southern Africa flourishes in gold trade. **1380** Kongo kingdom begins in the Congo River region of Zaire.	**c. 1420** Portuguese sailors explore west coast of Africa. **1468** Sanghai Empire dominates central Sudan in Africa.	
Asia	**c. 1000** Indian mathematician Sridhara recognizes the importance of zero. **c. 1000** Chinese begin to use gunpowder for warfare. **1041** Chinese printer Pi Sheng invents moveable type.	**c. 1100** Chinese explain the causes of solar and lunar eclipses. **1100s** Sultan of Baghdad probably the first to use pigeons for mail system. **1191** Tea arrives in Japan from China.	**1206** Genghis Khan unites the Mongols. **1232** Chinese build first rockets, which resembled fireworks. **1259-1260** Important astronomical observatories are built in Maragha, Iran, and Beijing, China.	**c. 1300** Ottoman dynasty begins in Turkey. **1368** Ming dynasty begins in China. **c. 1390** Ottoman Turks conquer Asia Minor.	**1419-1450** Korea prospers under King Sejong. **1448-1488** Thailand expands under King Trailok. **c. 1498** Portuguese sailor Vasco de Gama reaches India.	
Australia and Oceania	**c. 1000** Maoris settle in present-day New Zealand, where they hunt and gather.	**1100s** Polynesians establish settlements on the island of Pitcairn.	**c. 1200** On Tonga, Tui Tonga monarchy builds coral platform for worship.	**1350** Maoris prosper on New Zealand's North Island.	**c. 1400** Tonga people build a ceremonial center at Mu'a in the South Pacific.	

1500-1600	1600-1700	1700-1800	1800-1900	1900-2000
1500s Europeans explore North America and claim land for their countries. **1519-1521** Hernando Cortés of Spain conquers the Aztecs. **1534** French explorer Jacques Cartier travels to Canada. **1540s** Spanish come to California.	**1607** English establish first permanent colony in North America at Jamestown, Virginia. **1608** Québec founded by French settlers. **1619** First African slaves brought to North America. **1625** Dutch found New Amsterdam (later called New York).	**1775** American Revolution begins. **1776** Declaration of Independence approved. **1792** New York Stock Exchange is organized. **1793** Eli Whitney invents cotton gin. **1796** Edward Jenner develops smallpox vaccine.	**1804** Lewis and Clark begin exploring route to Pacific Ocean. **1861-1865** U.S. Civil War. **1863** Lincoln issues the Emancipation Proclamation. **1876** Alexander Graham Bell invents the telephone.	**1908** Ford Motor Company produces first Model "T" automobile. **1960s** Martin Luther King, Jr. leads civil rights protests in U.S. **1969** Moon landing. **1979** Sandinistas take control of Nicaragua. **1990** Launch of Hubble Space Telescope.
1533 Francisco Pizarro of Spain conquers the Inca empire in South America.	**1608** Jesuits establish state of Paraguay. **1654** Portuguese drive Dutch from Brazil.	**1726** Spanish found city of Montevideo in Uruguay. **1727** Coffee first planted in Brazil. **1742** Native Americans of Peru rebel against Spaniards. **1763** Rio de Janeiro becomes Brazil's capital.	**1810** Simón Bolívar emerges to lead Latin American revolutions. **1825** Bolívar founds state of Bolivia. **1828** Uruguay becomes independent. **1879-1884** Chile, Peru, Bolivia at war. **1891** Civil war in Chile.	**1955** Military officials seize power from Argentinian president Peron. **1982** Falklands war between Argentina and Britain.
1506-1507 First maps of the New World are printed in Europe. **1519** Ferdinand Magellan sets sail from Spain to circumnavigate the globe. **1514-1565** Explorers introduce pineapples, coffee, chocolate, sweet potatoes, corn, and tobacco to Europe.	**1608** Galileo makes astronomical observations using newly invented telescope. **1628** William Harvey describes the circulation of blood in the body. **1687** Isaac Newton describes the fundamental laws of motion.	**1715** Daniel Fahrenheit develops first mercury thermometer. **1742** Anders Celsius creates thermometer marking 0° as freezing and 100° as boiling. **1789** French Revolution begins.	**1804** Napoleon becomes emperor of the French. **1859** Charles Darwin publishes book about the evolution of species. **1884** Greenwich, England established as the zero meridian for time zones. **1896** Italian Marconi invents wireless telegraph.	**1914-1918** World War I. **1916** Albert Einstein publishes his General Theory of Relativity. **1928** Alexander Fleming discovers penicillin. **1939-1945** World War II. **1989** Berlin Wall, built in 1961, is torn down. **1990** East and West Germany are united.
1530s Slave trade begins, organized by the Portuguese. **1562** African slaves are sent to the Americas as the English slave trade begins.	**c. 1650** Ethiopia expels Portuguese missionaries and diplomats. **1652** Dutch establish Cape Town in South Africa. **1680s** Asante kingdom rises in West Africa. **1686** Louis XIV of France annexes Madagascar.	**c. 1710** The 300-year-old African Kingdom of Kongo collapses after Portuguese invasion. **1724-1734** African leaders stop slave trade in West Africa. **1740s** Slave trade resumes. **1755** Sailors bring first outbreak of smallpox to Cape Town.	**1822** Liberia founded as home for freed U.S. slaves. **1830** French invade Algeria. **1873-1874** Asante and British at war. **1879** Zulu and British at war. **1880s** Nearly all of Africa is colonized by European countries.	**1931** Railway from Angola to Mozambique completed. **1963** Organization of African Unity founded. **1980** Zimbabwe is the last African country to gain independence from colonial rule. **1990** Nelson Mandela elected president of South Africa.
1520-1566 Ottoman Empire at its peak. **1526** Mongols invade India, establishing Mogul Empire. **1533** Ivan the Terrible rules as the first tsar of Russia.	**1630s** Japan expels most foreigners, allowing trade only with the Dutch and Chinese. **1644** Manchus invade China, establish the Quing dynasty.	**1735-1795** Chinese empire reaches its furthest extent. **1763** Britain becomes dominant power in India. **1783-1788** Japan experiences severe famine. **1784** U.S. begins trade with China.	**1804** Russia attempts but fails to establish trade with Japan. **1854** U.S. opens Japan to trade. **1857** Native soldiers in India rebel against English rulers. **1872** First Japanese railway opens.	**1900** Boxer Rebellion in China. **1917** Bolshevik Revolution in Russia. **1920** In India, Gandhi leads a peaceful non-cooperation movement. **1939-1945** World War II. **1957** Russians launch Sputnik space satellite. **1965-1973** Vietnam War.
1526 Portuguese land on Papua New Guinea. **1550s** Maoris in New Zealand build fortified enclosures.	**1600s** Dutch sailors discover the north and west coasts of Australia by accident. **1642-1644** Abel Tasman explores Tasmania and New Zealand.	**1768-1771** British Captain James Cook's first voyage to the Pacific. **1788** British begin to settle Australia with prisoners, creating a penal colony.	**1801-1803** Matthew Flinders circumnavigates and names Australia. **1851** Gold found in southeastern Australia.	**1901** British colonies become states, form the Commonwealth of Australia. **1933** Australia takes control of a large part of Antarctica. **2000** Sydney, Australia the site of the Summer Olympic Games.

The Basics of Maps and Cartography

What is a Map?

A map is a picture–or representation–of a place. Most maps are drawn to show places from above. When you think of maps, you might picture a folded road map or a wall map that hangs in the classroom. But, there are many different kinds of maps. Satellite images, or pictures of Earth taken from space, are maps. Floor plans of houses are maps too, because they show where each room is. In fact, you probably keep a lot of maps in your head. These "mental" maps help you remember how to get to school or your friend's house without needing to ask directions every time.

This satellite image of the San Francisco Bay area clearly shows the shape of the coastline.

An atlas is a book of maps. In 1570, Abraham Ortelius developed the first modern atlas, although he didn't call it by that name. Another man, Gerardus Mercator, first used the term "atlas" in 1589 when he named his collection of maps after a person from mythology named Atlas. In Greek mythology, Atlas was forced to support the world on his shoulders as punishment for warring against the gods. Although the word "atlas" is still used to mean a book of maps, atlases today may contain diagrams, tables, and text, in addition to maps.

Atlas

People who make maps are called "mapmakers" or "cartographers." Cartography is the art of making maps. The word comes from the Latin **carta**, meaning "map" and the Greek **graph** meaning "write."

On this road map of San Francisco, you can get information on street names and points of interest.

Lines of latitude and longitude intersect on a globe to form a grid.

History of Mapmaking

Thousands of years ago, ancient people developed the first maps as they explored new places and settled new lands. The Chinese, the Arabs, and the Indians were among the first people to experiment with mapmaking, creating maps by drawing on animal skins and rocks, and by carving maps on stones and in wood. In Babylon, an ancient Middle Eastern civilization, people carved maps into stone tablets. Ancient Egyptians drew maps on papyrus (a plant made into paper) and carved them into temple walls. Several thousand years ago, Europeans drew maps on paper, using the maps to help find their way across oceans to new lands and then to guide them home safely.

Ancient Greeks made and used globes, which are three-dimensional models of Earth. The Greeks divided the globe into segments, using lines of latitude and longitude. Later, these lines were overlaid onto flat maps. Today we still use latitude and longitude to find places on globes and maps.

This map, drawn in 1587, shows what North and South America were thought to look like at the time.

Major Types of Maps

Political Maps

Many of the maps you see are political maps. Political maps show how people have divided up the land on Earth. Using different colors, political maps show the borders between countries, states, provinces, and territories. The maps also show the location of cities, which are represented by different size type to indicate populations, roads, parks, and other features.

Physical Maps

Physical maps use different colors to show the elevation, or height, of land and the depth of water on the surface of the earth. Physical maps help readers see mountains, valleys, oceans, lakes, and rivers. Each physical map has its own legend, which explains which colors represent various elevations of land and depths of water.

Thematic Maps

Thematic maps use different colors to give information about specific themes or topics, such as populations, climates, languages spoken, or economies in different parts of the world. You can use thematic maps to compare and contrast information on one map or between several maps. Like physical maps, each thematic map has its own legend.

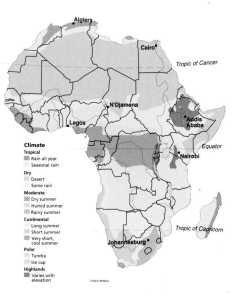

Locator Maps

Locator maps are small, simple maps that show what continent, region, or state is featured on a more detailed map. Locators point out where the maps are in relation to a larger area.

Maps Today

During the past 50 years, mapping around the world has become very precise. Sophisticated computers use information taken from satellite images—photos of Earth taken from space—and other sources to produce highly accurate maps used by people in business, government, and education. Students use maps to learn about foreign countries. Business people use maps to decide where to sell new products. And governmental agencies, like local fire and police departments, use maps to pinpoint houses and their residents who may need assistance.

Maps are available in a variety of places and formats. In addition to reading paper maps, you can use maps on your computer—with special mapping software or on the Internet. If you'd like to see and use a special set of Rand McNally digital maps—for homework or just for fun—you can access our special kids' Web site at:

randmcnallykids.com

How to Use This Atlas

By definition, an atlas is a book of maps. Therefore, to use an atlas you need to understand a few things about reading maps. The sections below explain how to use the maps in this atlas, as well as other parts of the book.

Finding Places

Finding places in an atlas is an adventure–a journey that takes you across rivers, over mountains, and into new countries. To find places in the Rand McNally's *Children's Millennium® Atlas of the World*, use the following tools:

Index Map

At the very front of the book is an index map. The index map shows each of the seven continents in a different color, and it lists the pages where you'll find the maps for each continent.

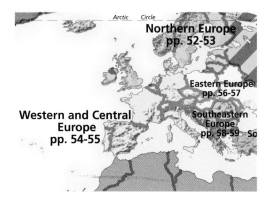

Index

At the very back of the book is the index–a list of the many places (such as cities, towns, and countries) and features (such as mountains and rivers) shown on the maps. The index tells you the page where you'll find each place or feature, and it also includes a letter-and-number code that tells you exactly where to look on the map to find the place or feature.

Map Grids

To help you locate places and features, each map includes a "map grid" along its four sides. Along the left and right sides are letters, and along the top and bottom sides are numbers. The letter-and-number codes in the index correspond to the letters and numbers along the sides of the maps.

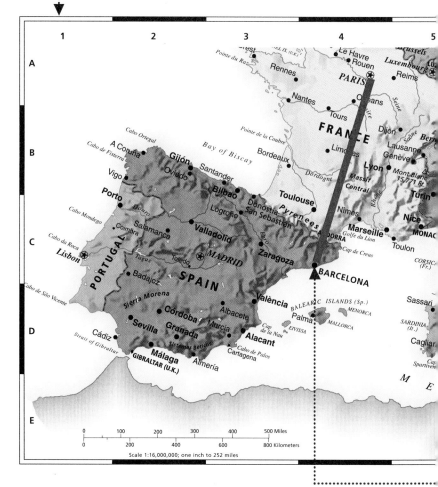

Latitude/Longitude

Imaginary lines that run vertically from the top of the earth to the bottom are called lines of longitude. These lines, which meet at the top of the earth and at the bottom, are also called meridians. The imaginary lines that run horizontally around the globe are called lines of latitude. These lines, which are parallel to one another and therefore never meet, are also known as parallels. The equator, which runs around the very middle of the earth, is the best known line of latitude.

These imaginary lines of longitude and latitude cross and form grids, which help you find places on a map or globe. In this atlas, the equator, the Tropic of Cancer, and the Tropic of Capricorn–all lines of latitude–are shown.

Knowing Direction

Each of the maps in this atlas includes something called a compass rose–a circle with arrows and the letters N, S, E, and W. These letters represent the four main points of a compass: North, South, East, and West. (On some old maps, the compass roses are beautifully illustrated and include so many direction points that they actually look like flowering roses!)

This is an example of an ornate compass rose.

Using the Legend

Maps contain all sorts of information. The legend, sometimes called the "map key," explains the symbols that appear on the maps. Symbols are icons that represent something else. For example, a black star in a circle is the symbol for a capital city. So in France, you'll find a ✷ next to Paris, the capital city. Other symbols on the maps represent rivers, lakes, mountain peaks, and borders between countries.

The main legend in this atlas is located below the index map in the very front of the book. The physical maps and thematic maps all have legends next to them, on the same page.

River   Fresh Lake   Salt Lake   Seasonal Lake

Understanding Terms

This atlas includes a glossary on page 104. In the glossary you will find explanations of many geographic terms used in the atlas.

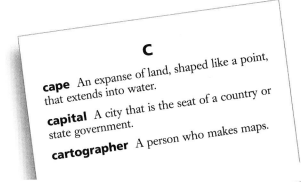

C

cape An expanse of land, shaped like a point, that extends into water.

capital A city that is the seat of a country or state government.

cartographer A person who makes maps.

Measuring Distance

Next to every map is a scale bar that shows how the size of the map relates to the real world. The scale bar also allows you to measure the distance between places. For example, let's say that one inch on a map scale represents about 250 miles in the real world, and that, using a ruler, you measured 2 inches between the cities of Paris, France, and Barcelona, Spain. Since one inch equals about 250 miles, then 2 inches must equal about 500 miles. This means that the distance between Paris and Barcelona in the real world is approximately 500 miles. Instead of using a ruler to measure distances, you can mark points along the edge of a piece of paper and then use the scale bar to measure the distance between the points.

| 0 | 100 | 200 | 300 | 400 | 500 Miles |
| 0 | 200 | 400 | 600 | 800 Kilometers |

Scale 1:16,000,000; one inch to 252 miles

Learning about Countries

If you want to learn some basic facts about any country, or to see what its flag looks like, turn to the Country Flag and Fact File that begins on page 96. This section shows each country's flag and lists its size, population, and capital city.

Togo
Area: 21,925 sq mi (56,785 sq km)
Population: 4,992,000
Capital: Lomé

World Climates

This map shows the climate zones of the world. Climate describes the weather conditions that occur in an area over a long period of time–not weeks and months, but years. The legend to the right of the map shows the specific climates that you can find on the map.

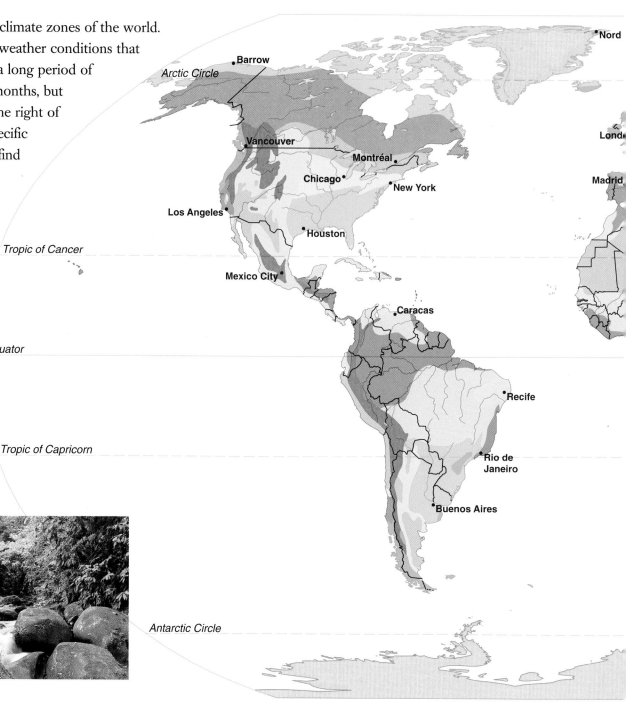

Climates are created by temperature and precipitation (rain, snow), and climates around the world vary for different reasons. In general, Earth's climates grow hotter as you approach the equator, and become colder as you move north or south from the equator. This is because the Sun's rays hit Earth most directly and most often in the tropics–the area between the Tropic of Cancer and the Tropic of Capricorn. Also, climates tend to be cooler in areas with high elevations because the thinner air high up holds less heat. Finally, areas that lie along the coast of an ocean or sea often have climates much milder than that of inland areas, thanks to ocean breezes and currents.

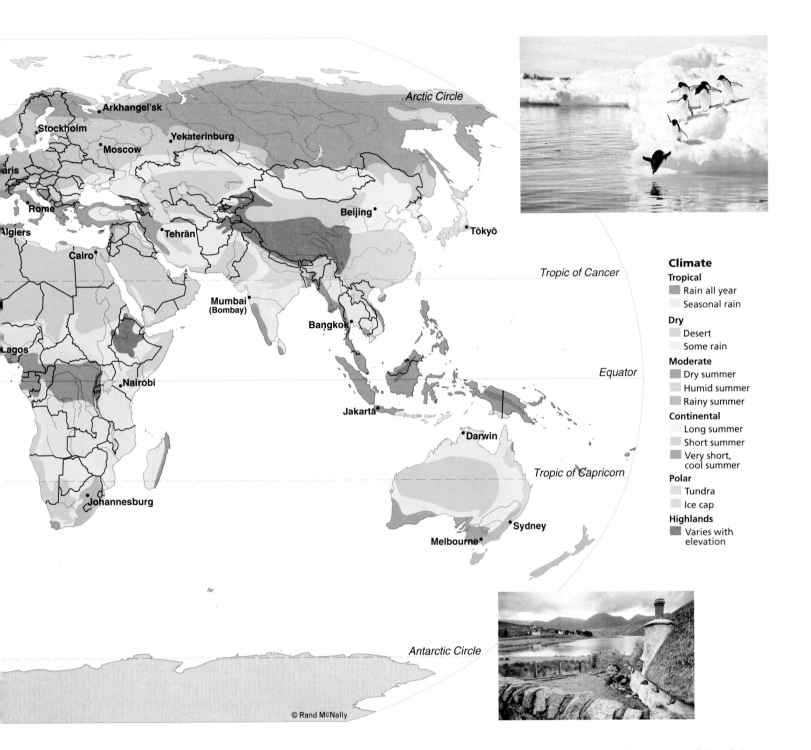

Arctic Circle

Arkhangel'sk

Stockholm

Yekaterinburg

Moscow

Paris

Rome

Algiers

Beijing

Tehrān

Tōkyō

Cairo

Tropic of Cancer

Mumbai
(Bombay)

Lagos

Bangkok

Equator

Nairobi

Jakarta

Darwin

Tropic of Capricorn

Johannesburg

Sydney

Melbourne

Antarctic Circle

© Rand McNally

Climate

Tropical
- Rain all year
- Seasonal rain

Dry
- Desert
- Some rain

Moderate
- Dry summer
- Humid summer
- Rainy summer

Continental
- Long summer
- Short summer
- Very short, cool summer

Polar
- Tundra
- Ice cap

Highlands
- Varies with elevation

Precipitation is the other factor that determines climate. Usually, areas of heaviest precipitation are found along the equator, where warm tropical air holds the greatest amount of water vapor. The reddish colors on the map show areas that experience tropical climates: the great rain forests of northern South America, central Africa, and Indonesia.

The terrain, or physical features, of an area also affects precipitation. When the terrain blocks the flow of breezes, it can dramatically alter the pattern of rainfall. Tall mountain ranges force moist air currents to rise above them, and when the air descends on the other side of the mountain, it releases moisture in the form of heavy rains. This "rainshadow effect"–where one side of a mountain

range receives abundant rainfall and the other is desert–can be observed in the northwestern United States and in Chile west and east of the Andes.

The climate we live in directly affects our lifestyles. The type of clothing we wear, the foods we eat, the way we travel, and the home we inhabit–all are dictated by climate.

World Economies

This map identifies economic activity around the world. The colors of the different areas on the map explain how most of the people in a particular area make their living.

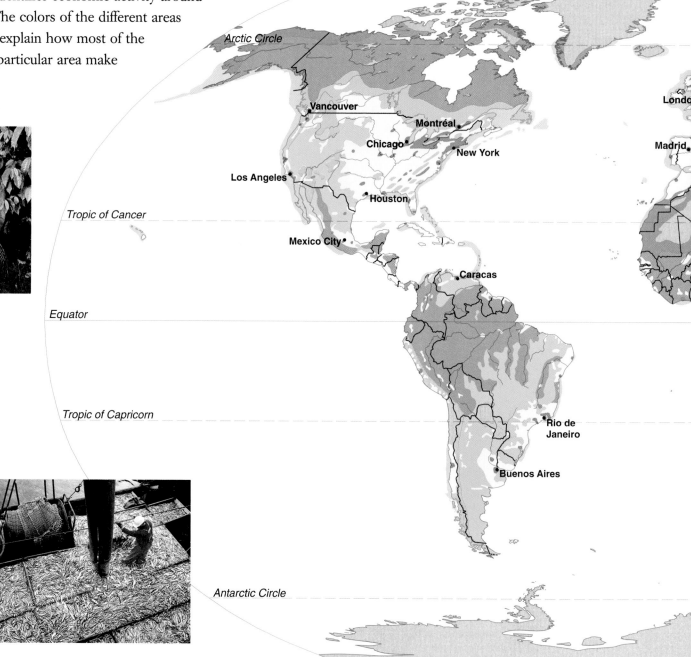

The physical characteristics of the land, such as fertile valleys and oil-rich plains, determine how people are able to use it and make livings. Compare this map to the World Physical map on pages 20-21. In general, areas where farming takes place (shown in yellow on this World Economies map) contain some of Earth's most fertile soils. Food harvested from the wide plains and river valleys of Europe, southeastern Asia, and central North America feeds much of the world's population. In some countries, such as India and China, agriculture is the major way to earn a living. In Brazil and the countries of eastern Europe, however, a much smaller part of the work force raises crops. This fraction is even smaller in Canada, the United States, and western Europe.

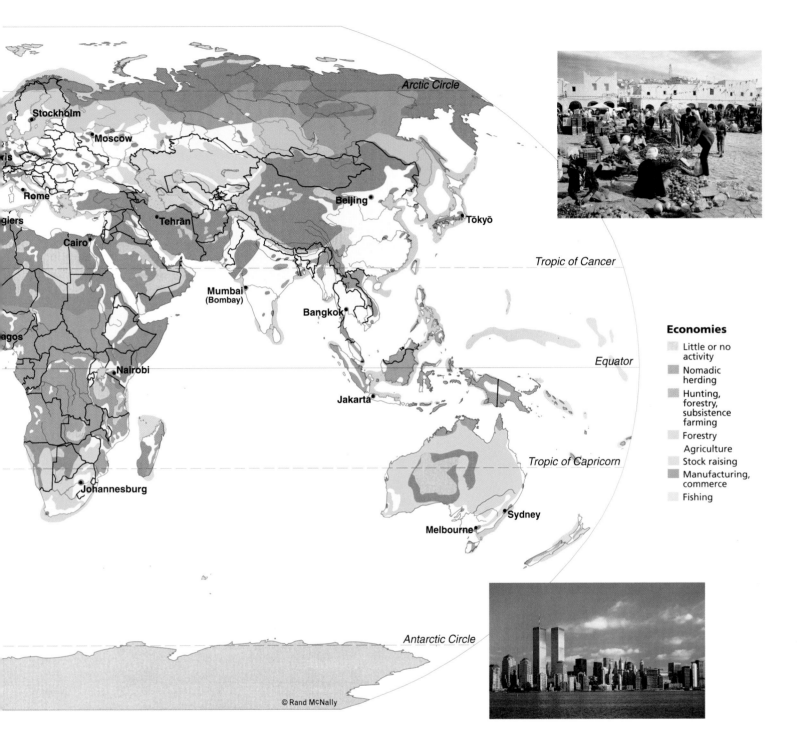

Stockholm

Moscow

Rome

Algiers

Cairo

Tehrān

Beijing

Tōkyō

Lagos

Nairobi

Mumbai
(Bombay)

Bangkok

Jakarta

Johannesburg

Melbourne

Sydney

Arctic Circle

Tropic of Cancer

Equator

Tropic of Capricorn

Antarctic Circle

© Rand McNally

Economies

- Little or no activity
- Nomadic herding
- Hunting, forestry, subsistence farming
- Forestry
- Agriculture
- Stock raising
- Manufacturing, commerce
- Fishing

Very few regions of the world are used for manufacturing and trade. These areas are sometimes called "developed." In the United States, for instance, developed areas grew near transportation routes and land that contained natural resources such as minerals. Major manufacturing centers such as Chicago and Montréal line the shores of the Great Lakes and the St. Lawrence Seaway, an important

transportation route that provides access to the Atlantic Ocean. Likewise, Germany's Ruhr Valley has long provided mineral resources, and the country's position in the center of Europe has helped it grow into a major industrial force.

In general, countries that are more economically developed have a greater range of industries than less developed countries. This is because people are able to specialize in the work that they do best, and use the money that they earn to pay for other goods and services that they need.

World Population

This map shows where people live in the world. The legend to the right of the map explains what the different colors mean in terms of population density. Population density is a measure of the number of people living in each square mile (2.59 square kilometers) of land.

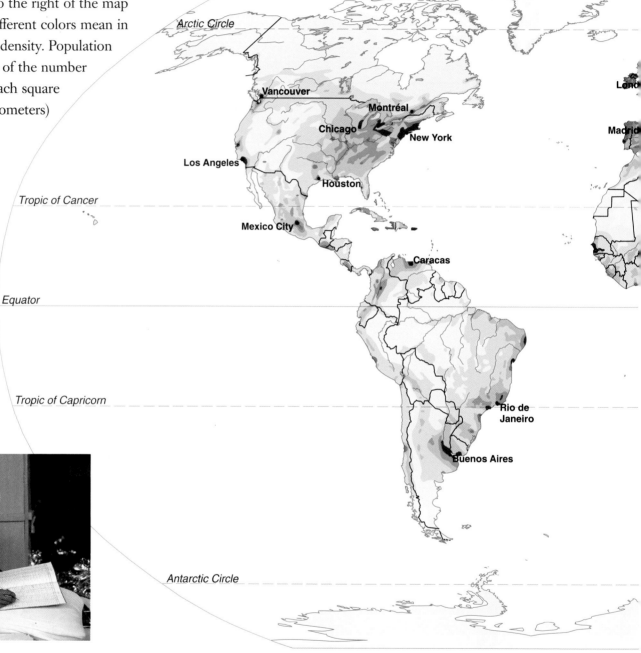

Population densities vary for many reasons, including climate and terrain. For example, the continent of Antarctica–Earth's coldest region–is uninhabited, meaning that no one lives there permanently. Its harsh climate makes living there nearly impossible.

Lands with favorable climates and terrains tend to be densely populated, especially if they are good for farming. The presence of the Nile River explains the ribbon of dense population that runs through the desert lands of Sudan and Egypt in northern Africa: People live and farm close to its fertile banks. In the vast rain forests of South America, people settle along the Amazon River.

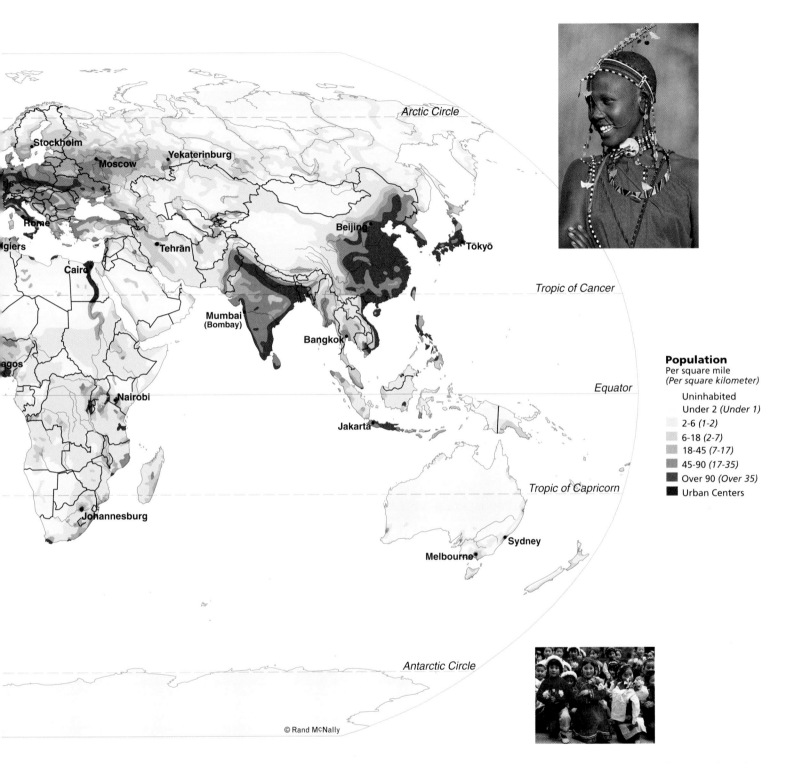

Arctic Circle

Stockholm
Moscow
Yekaterinburg
Rome
lgiers
Tehrān
Cairo
Beijing
Tōkyō

Tropic of Cancer

Mumbai
(Bombay)
Bangkok
agos
Nairobi

Equator

Jakarta

Johannesburg

Tropic of Capricorn

Sydney
Melbourne

Antarctic Circle

© Rand McNally

Population
Per square mile
(Per square kilometer)

Uninhabited
Under 2 *(Under 1)*
2-6 *(1-2)*
6-18 *(2-7)*
18-45 *(7-17)*
45-90 *(17-35)*
Over 90 *(Over 35)*
Urban Centers

Look for the red and purple regions—they represent the world's most densely populated areas. The huge populations of India and China are settled in Asia's rich farmlands. For the most part, most of these people still live away from cities in country, or rural, areas.

In Europe and the United States, by contrast, the most populous areas are cities, or urban areas, which grew up near farmland, resources, and trade routes, especially waterways. In the United States, people are concentrated along the Atlantic and Pacific Oceans, the shores of the Great Lakes, and the banks of the Mississippi River. Cities contain the majority of the population of Australia, Argentina, Canada, France, Japan, and the United States.

Japan is one of the world's most densely populated countries. Slightly smaller than the state of California, it holds more than 126 million people.

World Physical

This map shows the physical features found on the surface of the earth. The colors and shading on the map indicate the kind of terrain found in that area of the world. The legend to the right of the map explains what the colors mean.

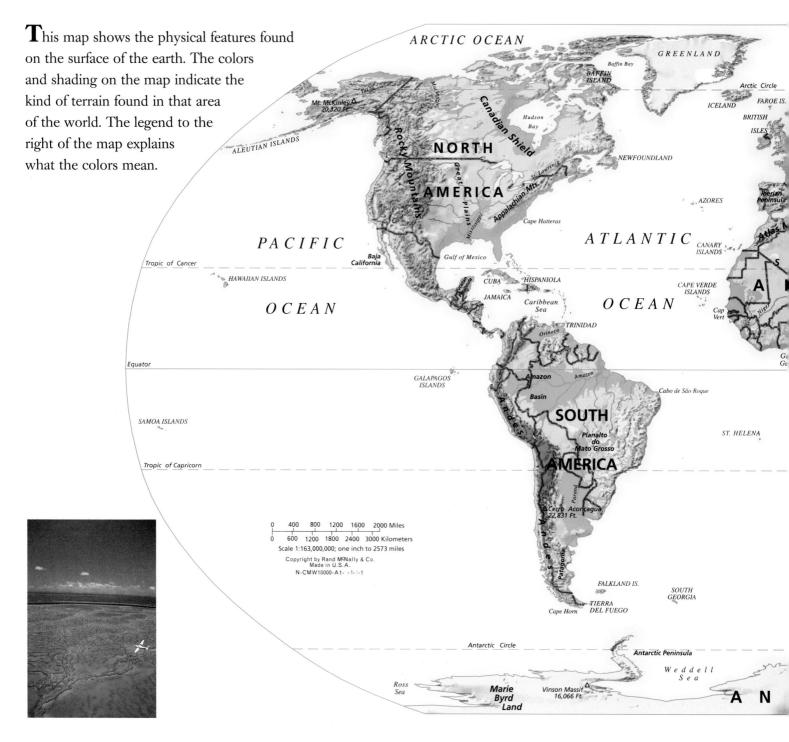

ARCTIC OCEAN
GREENLAND
Baffin Bay
BAFFIN ISLAND
Arctic Circle
ICELAND
FAROE IS.
BRITISH ISLES
Mt. McKinley 20,320 Ft.
Yukon
Mackenzie
Canadian Shield
Hudson Bay
ALEUTIAN ISLANDS
Rocky Mountains
NORTH AMERICA
Great Plains
NEWFOUNDLAND
St. Lawrence
Appalachian Mts.
AZORES
Iberian Peninsula
Atlas M
PACIFIC
Colorado
Cape Hatteras
ATLANTIC
CANARY ISLANDS
S
Tropic of Cancer
Baja California
Gulf of Mexico
A
HAWAIIAN ISLANDS
Yucatan Peninsula
CUBA
HISPANIOLA
JAMAICA
Caribbean Sea
CAPE VERDE ISLANDS
OCEAN
Cap Vert
Niger
OCEAN
OCEAN
TRINIDAD
Orinoco
G
Gu
Equator
GALAPAGOS ISLANDS
Amazon
Amazon
Cabo de São Roque
SAMOA ISLANDS
Andes
Basin
SOUTH
Planalto do Mato Grosso
ST. HELENA
Tropic of Capricorn
AMERICA
Parana
Cerro Aconcagua 22,831 Ft.
Andes
Patagonia
FALKLAND IS.
SOUTH GEORGIA
TIERRA DEL FUEGO
Cape Horn

0   400   800   1200   1600   2000 Miles
0   600   1200   1800   2400   3000 Kilometers
Scale 1:163,000,000; one inch to 2573 miles
Copyright by Rand McNally & Co.
Made in U.S.A.
N-CMW10000-A1- -1- 1-1

Antarctic Circle
Antarctic Peninsula
Weddell Sea
Ross Sea
Marie Byrd Land
Vinson Massif 16,066 Ft.
AN

More than three-quarters of Earth is covered by water, including four large oceans and many smaller seas, all made up of salt water. Fresh water–water without salt–is most often found in smaller inland lakes and rivers, such as the Great Lakes in North America.

The remaining part of Earth's surface is made up of landmasses with mountains, deserts, rivers, lakes, and plateaus. The floors of oceans and seas also have mountains and valleys, but you can't see them because they're underwater. This map shows the names and different categories of Earth's physical features.

Earth's surface is called the crust, a wrinkled layer of solid rock that is constantly changing. The crust is cracked into a dozen separate fragments called "tectonic plates," which float on a sea of dense, semi-liquid rock far below the surface. Columns of this molten rock slowly rise and fall, nudging the bases of the crustal plates that float on Earth's surface. As the plates try to move, they push into neighboring plates.

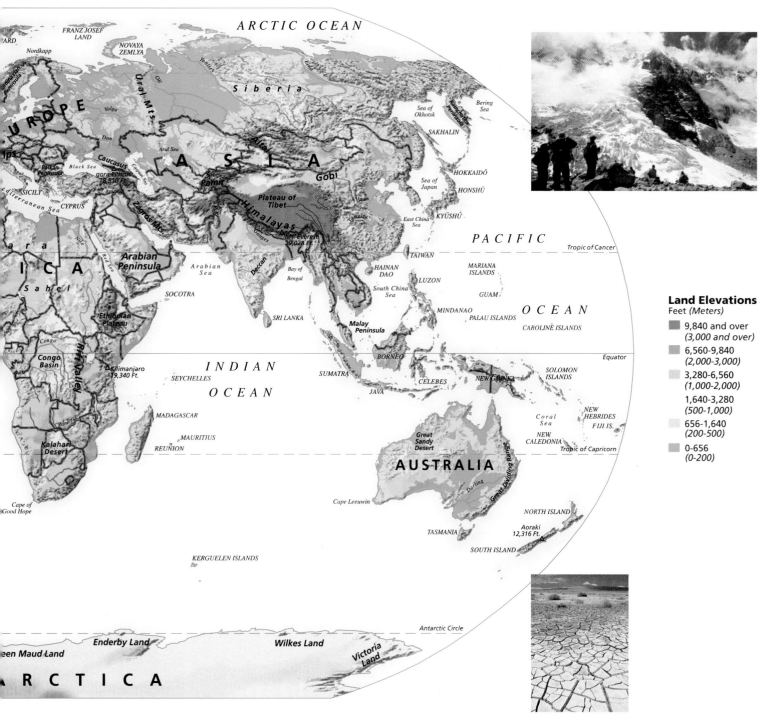

ARCTIC OCEAN

FRANZ JOSEF LAND

NOVAYA ZEMLYA

Nordkapp

Kola Peninsula

Yenisey

Siberia

Ob'

Lena

EUROPE

Volga

Ural Mts.

Don

Caucasus
gora Elbrus
18,510 Ft.

Black Sea

Aral Sea

Caspian Sea

ASIA

Amu

Pamir

Gobi

Bering Sea

Sea of Okhotsk

Kamchatka Peninsula

SAKHALIN

HOKKAIDŌ

Alps

Balkan Peninsula

SICILY

Mediterranean Sea

CYPRUS

Zagros Mts.

Plateau of Tibet

Himalayas

Ganges

Mt. Everest 29,028 Ft.

Huan

Yangtze

Sea of Japan

HONSHŪ

East China Sea

KYŪSHŪ

PACIFIC

Sahara

Nile

Red Sea

Arabian Peninsula

Arabian Sea

Decan

Bay of Bengal

TAIWAN

HAINAN DAO

MARIANA ISLANDS

Tropic of Cancer

AFRICA

Sahel

SOCOTRA

SRI LANKA

South China Sea

LUZON

GUAM

OCEAN

Ethiopian Plateau

Congo

Malay Peninsula

MINDANAO

PALAU ISLANDS

CAROLINE ISLANDS

Congo Basin

Rift Valley

Kilimanjaro 19,340 Ft.

SEYCHELLES

INDIAN

BORNEO

SUMATRA

CELEBES

JAVA

NEW GUINEA

SOLOMON ISLANDS

Equator

OCEAN

Coral Sea

NEW HEBRIDES

FIJI IS.

Zambezi

MADAGASCAR

MAURITIUS

REUNION

Kalahari Desert

Great Sandy Desert

AUSTRALIA

Darling

Great Dividing Range

NEW CALEDONIA

Tropic of Capricorn

Cape of Good Hope

Cape Leeuwin

TASMANIA

NORTH ISLAND

Aoraki 12,316 Ft.

SOUTH ISLAND

KERGUELEN ISLANDS

Antarctic Circle

Enderby Land

Wilkes Land

Victoria Land

Queen Maud Land

ANTARCTICA

Land Elevations
Feet (Meters)

- 9,840 and over (3,000 and over)
- 6,560-9,840 (2,000-3,000)
- 3,280-6,560 (1,000-2,000)
- 1,640-3,280 (500-1,000)
- 656-1,640 (200-500)
- 0-656 (0-200)

Over millions of years, the pushing, grinding, and colliding of tectonic plates has crumpled, folded, and lifted rock, slowly building up the world's great mountain ranges. For instance, the Appalachian Mountains in eastern North America resulted from a collision between North America and Africa some 320 million years ago. Likewise,

the Himalayas–the highest mountains in the world–were forced upward when India rammed into Asia. On this map, you can see where Earth's mountains have formed.

The map also shows the world's desert regions. Deserts are dry lands with low rainfall and sparse plant and animal life. Not all deserts are hot, sandy, and sunny. They can also be cold, rocky, or ice-covered.

World Political

This map shows the countries of the world. Unlike the other maps in this section, the map colors do not tell you anything about a particular country. They are there to make it easier to see each country separately on the map. This type of map is called a political map because it shows the world's divisions by country.

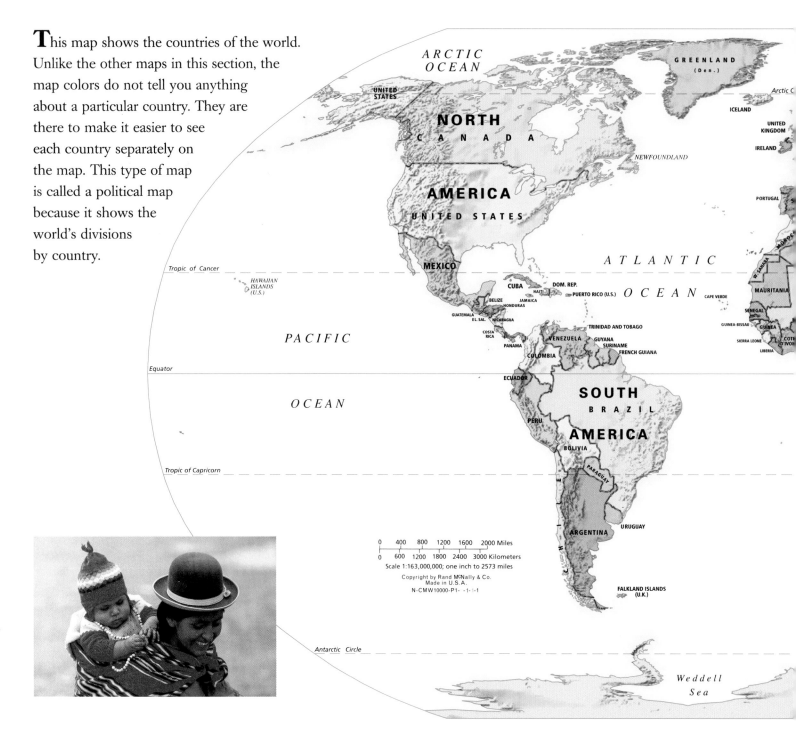

International boundaries are represented on this map by a dashed black line. These lines divide the world into separate countries. Sometimes country borders follow natural features such as rivers or mountain ranges. For example, the crooked northwestern border of China runs along a river. In many places, though, people decide where boundaries should fall–as with the straight portion of the boundary between Canada and the United States.

Although most political boundaries are well established, changes still occur. In 1990, for instance, East and West Germany reunited, and Germany became a single country. In 1991 the Soviet Union dissolved, and its 15 republics all became independent countries.

Some countries, like Russia and Canada, are large and take up a lot of space on any world political map. Other countries–like Vatican City in Rome, Italy– are so tiny that they aren't usually shown on a world political map unless the map scale is very large.

ARCTIC OCEAN

SWEDEN
NORWAY
FINLAND
EST.
LAT.
LITH.
GER. POLAND BELARUS
EUROPE UKRAINE
AUS. HUNG.
ROM.
ITALY ALB.
GREECE TURKEY
TUNISIA CYPRUS LEB.
ISRAEL SYRIA
JORDAN IRAQ
LIBYA EGYPT
NIGER CHAD SUDAN
AFRICA
NIGERIA CENTRAL
CAMEROON AFRICAN REPUBLIC
GUINEA
GABON CONGO DEM. REP. KENYA
OF THE UGANDA
CONGO TANZANIA
ANGOLA ZAMBIA MALAWI
NAMIBIA ZIMBABWE
BOTSWANA MOZAMBIQUE
SWAZILAND
SOUTH LESOTHO
AFRICA

RUSSIA
KAZAKHSTAN MONGOLIA
ASIA
UZBEKISTAN KYRG.
TURKMENISTAN TAJIK.
GEO. AZER. CHINA
AFGHANISTAN
IRAN
PAKISTAN
SAUDI QATAR
ARABIA U.A.E.
OMAN
YEMEN
ERITREA
DJIBOUTI
ETHIOPIA
SOMALIA

NORTH
KOREA
SOUTH JAPAN
KOREA

NEPAL
INDIA BANG.
MYANMAR LAOS
THAILAND VIETNAM
CAMB.
SRI LANKA
MALAYSIA
INDONESIA

TAIWAN

PHILIPPINES

PAPUA
NEW GUINEA
SOLOMON
ISLANDS
FIJI

NEW
CALEDONIA
(Fr.)

AUSTRALIA

NEW ZEALAND

PACIFIC
OCEAN
Tropic of Cancer
Equator
Tropic of Capricorn

INDIAN
OCEAN

SVALBARD
(Norway)

Antarctic Circle

ANTARCTICA

When people study the world, they often group countries by land areas called continents. The seven continents are the great divisions of Earth's land. Nearly all of them are landmasses almost completely surrounded by water.

This atlas divides the world into the seven continents: North America, South America, Europe, Africa, Asia, Australia (including the South Pacific area of Oceania), and Antarctica.

NORTH AMERICA

North America stretches from Greenland in the Arctic Ocean to Panama on the Caribbean Sea. The far northern areas of the world's third-largest continent are permanently covered with ice and snow. Flat, fertile plains spread across the center. In the west rise the rugged chains of mountains that include the towering Rocky Mountains and Coast Ranges, and in the east are the ancient, rolling Appalachian Mountains. Deserts dominate the southwest, and tropical rain forests flourish near the equator.

North America is a continent of spectacular scenery, varied landscapes, and vast resources. It includes the Canadian Shield, where Earth's oldest rock lies; the glacier-gouged Great Lakes; the breathtaking Grand Canyon; the endless expanses of Mexico's white-sand beaches, and the lush volcanic islands of the Caribbean.

New York (above) is the largest city in the United States; El Castillo (left) at Chichen Itza, Mexico, represents ancient Mayan architecture; the lofty Alaska Range (below) soars above clouds in Denali National Park.

ARCTIC OCEAN

Arctic Circle

ALEUTIAN ISLANDS
Bering Sea
Bering Strait
Point Hope
Point Barrow

Beaufort Sea
Cape Bathurst

QUEEN ELIZABETH ISLANDS

ELLESMERE ISLAND

Kap Morris Jesup

GREENLAND (Denmark)

Kap Bridsten

Arctic Circle

Baffin Bay
Cape Adair

Ice Cap

Kap Mosting

Brooks Range
U.S.
Yukon
Kuskokwim
Anchorage
Alaska Range
Mt. McKinley 20,320 Ft.
Alaska Peninsula
Gulf of Alaska
Mt. Logan 19,551 Ft.

DEVON ISLAND
BANKS ISLAND

VICTORIA ISLAND

Great Bear Lake

Mackenzie

BAFFIN ISLAND

Foxe Basin

Cape Mercy

Kap Farvel

QUEEN CHARLOTTE ISLANDS
VANCOUVER ISLAND

Whitehorse

Great Slave Lake

Peace

Lake Athabasca

Hudson Bay

Churchill

Péninsule d'Ungava

NEWFOUNDLAND

Coast Mountains

Rocky Mountains

C A N A D A

Cascade Range

Cape Blanco
Cape Mendocino

Vancouver

Columbia

Edmonton

Saskatchewan

Canadian Shield

Lake Winnipeg

Nelson

James Bay

Smallwood Resevoir

Gulf of St. Lawrence

PACIFIC OCEAN

Coast Ranges

Sierra Nevada

Great Basin

Snake

Great Salt Lake

Albany

Great Plains

Lake Superior

Great Lakes

Lake Michigan

St. Lawrence

MONTRÉAL
Ottawa

Cape Sable

Mt. Whitney 14,494 Ft.

Colorado Plateau

Colorado

Denver

UNITED STATES

Missouri

CHICAGO

Lake Huron

L. Ontario
Niagara Falls
Lake Erie

Appalachian Mts.

NEW YORK

Washington

LOS ANGELES

Arkansas

Red

Ozark Plateau

Ohio

Cape Cod

Cape Hatteras

Mississippi

Coastal Plain

ATLANTIC OCEAN

Gulf of California

Baja California

Punta Eugenia

Cabo San Lucas

HOUSTON

Rio Grande

Cape Canaveral

BAHAMAS

Tropic of Cancer

MEXICO

Sierra Madre Occidental

Tropic of Cancer

GULF OF MEXICO

Cape Sable

Miami

Havana

CUBA

WEST INDIES

DOMINICAN REPUBLIC

LESSER ANTILLES

ISLAS REVILLAGIGEDO

MEXICO CITY

Bahía de Campeche

Pico de Orizaba 18,406 Ft.

Yucatan Peninsula

Canal de Yucatán

GREATER ANTILLES

HAITI

JAMAICA

PUERTO RICO (U.S.)

TRINIDAD AND TOBAGO

Sierra Madre Oriental

BELIZE

GUATEMALA

Gulf of Honduras

HONDURAS

CARIBBEAN SEA

EL SALVADOR

NICARAGUA
Lago de Nicaragua

COSTA RICA

Istmo de Panamá

PANAMA

Golfo de Panamá

Land Elevation
Feet (Meters)

- 9,840 and over (3,000 and over)
- 6,560 - 9,840 (2,000 - 3,000)
- 3,280 - 6,560 (1,000 - 2,000)
- 1,640 - 3,280 (500 - 1,000)
- 656 - 1,640 (200 - 500)
- 0 - 656 feet (0 - 200)

0 200 400 600 Miles
0 200 400 600 800 1000 Kilometers

Scale 1:45,000,000; one inch to 710 miles

Copyright by Rand McNally & Co.
Made in U.S.A.

N-CMW20000-A1- -1-:-1

N
W E
S

North America Facts

Area: 9,500,000 square miles (24,700,000 square kilometers)

Highest Mountain: Mount McKinley, Alaska, United States, 20,320 feet (6,194 meters)

Lowest Point: Death Valley, California, United States, -282 feet (-86 meters)

Longest River: Mississippi-Missouri, central United States, 3,740 miles (6,019 kilometers)

Largest Lake: Lake Superior, Canada-United States 31,700 square miles (82,100 square kilometers)

Largest Desert: Chihuahuan Desert, Mexico-United States, 175,000 square miles (453,000 square kilometers)

Largest Island: Greenland, 840,000 square miles (2,175,600 square kilometers)—*world's largest island*

THE LAND

North America is a land of abundance. The continent has plentiful minerals, mighty rivers that provide hydroelectric power, and rich farmland that yields fruits, vegetables and grain. The United States is the economic powerhouse of the continent, while Canada's economy is also diversified with mining, agriculture, and tourism. Mexico's oil fields are one of that country's most important resources. The countries of Central America export a variety of tropical produce to lands farther north.

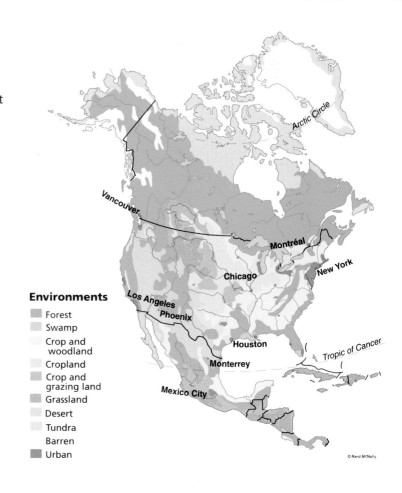

Environments

- Forest
- Swamp
- Crop and woodland
- Cropland
- Crop and grazing land
- Grassland
- Desert
- Tundra
- Barren
- Urban

© Rand McNally

Steel production in the United States and Canada is one of North America's best-known industries.

Industry

Industry provides a huge portion of the wealth in North America. Most industrial regions developed around port cities, where it was easy to receive raw materials and to ship out finished products. Mexico's role in manufacturing is growing as companies from the United States relocate their factories there. Canada and the United States, however, are still the leading industrial countries in North America.

Farming

North America produces more of the world's food than any other continent. In the temperate region that extends from southern Canada to northern Mexico, major crops include corn, wheat, and soybeans. Tropical and subtropical regions export bananas, cocoa, coffee, oranges, and other produce.

Environments

Forests, North America's dominant environment, cover one-third of the continent. Much of the land in the continent's midsection, especially the plains that lie between the Rocky Mountains and the Appalachian Mountains, is devoted to farming and livestock. Parched, barren deserts stretch across large parts of the southwestern United States and northwestern Mexico. Tundra spreads across most of Alaska and northern Canada. A thick sheet of ice covers nearly the entire island of Greenland. In contrast, the islands of the Caribbean support lush vegetation and dense tropical forests.

The midwestern United States is one of the world's largest producers of corn.

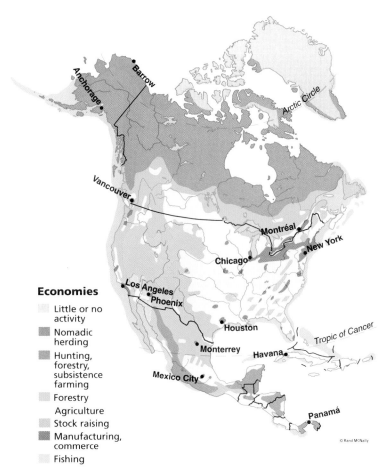

Economies

Little or no activity

Nomadic herding

Hunting, forestry, subsistence farming

Forestry

Agriculture

Stock raising

Manufacturing, commerce

Fishing

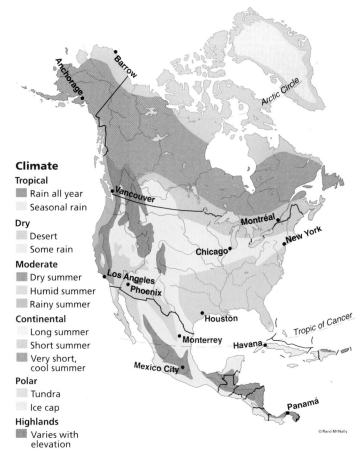

Climate

Tropical
Rain all year
Seasonal rain

Dry
Desert
Some rain

Moderate
Dry summer
Humid summer
Rainy summer

Continental
Long summer
Short summer
Very short, cool summer

Polar
Tundra
Ice cap

Highlands
Varies with elevation

Economies

North America's abundant resources provide both the continent and the world with food, raw materials such as wood and mineral ores, and manufactured goods.

Climate

Almost every type of climate is found in North America, from the frozen tundra in the far north to the tropical areas in the south. Much of the continent, however, enjoys a temperate climate that is just right for growing crops and raising cattle.

Mining and Mineral Resources

Much of the world's copper, lead, iron ore, and zinc are mined in North America. Coal, oil, and natural gas are plentiful, providing fuel for the factories of Canada, the United States, and Mexico.

Coal miners wear headlamps and protective gear when they work underground.

A logger loads cut timber onto a truck for transport.

Forestry

Canada is one of the world's major exporters of wood and wood products. Forestry also plays a major role in the economies of the Pacific Northwest, the Gulf Coast, and the southern Atlantic coastal regions of the United States.

THE PEOPLE

North America is a land settled by immigrants. Even the earliest North American Indians migrated from Asia across a land bridge that once linked the two continents. Today, much of the population is descended from Europeans; African Americans, many of whose ancestors were brought to North America as slaves from the sixteenth to the nineteenth centuries, are also an important part of North America's ethnic mix. North Americans speak Spanish and English primarily; French is spoken in the Canadian province of Québec. Many other native languages are also spoken throughout the continent. The United States has the largest population of any country in North America, and Mexico City is the continent's most populous city.

Three cowboys in Mexico City prepare to ride in a rodeo.

Children laugh on a playground in Cuba.

The Inuit people of Alaska and northern Canada build igloos with blocks of ice or compacted snow.

Montréal, Canada, has a distinctly French character.

Los Angeles, California, reflects a "melting pot" of nationalities and cultures.

Three children row on a pond in New York's Central Park.

A costumed crowd gathers for a carnival on Antigua, an island in the Lesser Antilles.

ARCTIC OCEAN

Bering Sea

Point Hope

Arctic Circle

Point Barrow

Beaufort Sea

Cape Bathurst

Nome

ALEUTIAN ISLANDS

U.S.

Kuskokwim Fairbanks

Alaska Range Mt. McKinley 20,320 ft.

Anchorage

Mt. Logan 19,551 ft.

Gulf of Alaska

Juneau

Yukon

Mackenzie

QUEEN CHARLOTTE ISLANDS

VANCOUVER ISLAND

QUEEN ELIZABETH ISLANDS

BANKS ISLAND

VICTORIA ISLAND

ELLESMERE ISLAND

Kap Morris Jesup

GREENLAND (Denmark)

Kap Brewster

Arctic Circle

DEVON ISLAND

Baffin Bay

Cape Adair

Kap Meating

BAFFIN ISLAND

Kap Farvel

Cape Mercy

Godthåb

Great Bear Lake

Yellowknife

Great Slave Lake

Peace

CANADA

Churchill

Hudson Bay

Péninsule d'Ungava

NEWFOUNDLAND

St. John's

Rocky Mountains

Edmonton

Vancouver

Calgary

Regina

Saskatchewan

Lake Winnipeg

Nelson

Albany

Gulf of St. Lawrence

Cape Sable

Halifax

Seattle

Winnipeg

Thunder Bay

Quebec

MONTREAL

Columbia

Portland

Boise

Snake

Missouri

Lake Superior

Minneapolis

St. Paul

Milwaukee

CHICAGO

Lake Michigan

Ottawa

Toronto

Lake Huron

Lake Ontario

Buffalo

DETROIT

Cleveland

Lake Erie

Boston

Cape Cod

NEW YORK

PHILADELPHIA

Cape Blanco

Cape Mendocino

San Francisco

San Jose

Oakland

Sierra Nevada

Great Salt Lake

Salt Lake City

Great Basin

Omaha

Denver

Kansas City

St. Louis

Pittsburgh

Ohio

Louisville

Washington

Richmond

Norfolk

Appalachian Mts.

Mt. Whitney 14,494 ft.

Colorado

Arkansas

Wichita

Nashville

Charlotte

Cape Hatteras

ATLANTIC OCEAN

LOS ANGELES

SAN DIEGO

Albuquerque

Tulsa

Memphis

Atlanta

Tijuana

Phoenix

Red

DALLAS

Birmingham

Jacksonville

Tucson

El Paso

Fort Worth

Mississippi

Mobile

Punta Eugenia

Ciudad Juárez

San Antonio

Rio Grande

HOUSTON

New Orleans

Cape Canaveral

Sierra Madre Occidental

Chihuahua

Tampa

Cabo San Lucas

PACIFIC OCEAN

Gulf of California

MEXICO

MONTERREY

GULF OF MEXICO

Cape Sable

Miami

BAHAMAS

Tropic of Cancer

Tropic of Cancer

San Luis Potosí

Tampico

HAVANA

GREATER ANTILLES

CUBA

DOMINICAN REPUBLIC

PUERTO RICO (U.S.)

LESSER ANTILLES

GUADALAJARA

León

Mérida

Canal de Yucatán

HAITI

Port-au-Prince

SANTO DOMINGO

ISLAS REVILLAGIGEDO

MEXICO CITY

Veracruz

Bahía de Campeche

Yucatan Peninsula

JAMAICA

Kingston

PUEBLA

Pico de Orizaba 18,406 ft.

Acapulco

Sierra Madre Oriental

Belmopan

BELIZE

Gulf of Honduras

CARIBBEAN SEA

TRINIDAD AND TOBAGO

Guatemala

GUATEMALA

HONDURAS

Tegucigalpa

San Salvador

EL SALVADOR

NICARAGUA

Managua

Lago de Nicaragua

San José

Panamá

COSTA RICA

PANAMA

Golfo de Panamá

North America Facts

Population: 472,600,000

Population Density:
50 people per square mile
(19 per square kilometer)

Most Populous Country:
United States,
271,490,000 people

Largest City:
Mexico City, Mexico,
19,100,000 people
(metropolitan area)

0 200 400 600 Miles
0 200 400 600 800 1000 Kilometers
Scale 1:45,000,000; one inch to 710 miles
Copyright by Rand McNally & Co.
Made in U.S.A.
N-CMW20000-P1- -1-1-1

N
W E
S

Ottawa has been Canada's capital since 1857.

CANADA

Canada is the largest country in North America. A large portion of the land lies in the harsh regions of the far north, making it one of the most sparsely populated countries in the world. Most of Canada's people live in cities and towns near the country's border with the United States. In 1999, a new territory called Nunavut, which means "Our Land," was carved out of the eastern and northern portions of the Northwest Territories; it joined 10 provinces and two other territories. Most of the citizens of Nunavut are Inuit, the native people of northern Canada.

Totem poles are an integral part of Native American culture in western Canada.

On Prince Edward Island, a lighthouse stands at Shipwreck Point.

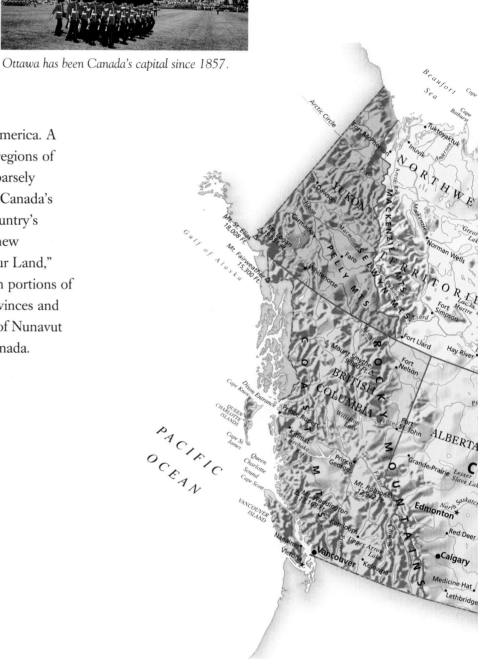

Polar bears roam the frozen wilderness of northern Canada.

10   11   12   13   14   15   16   17

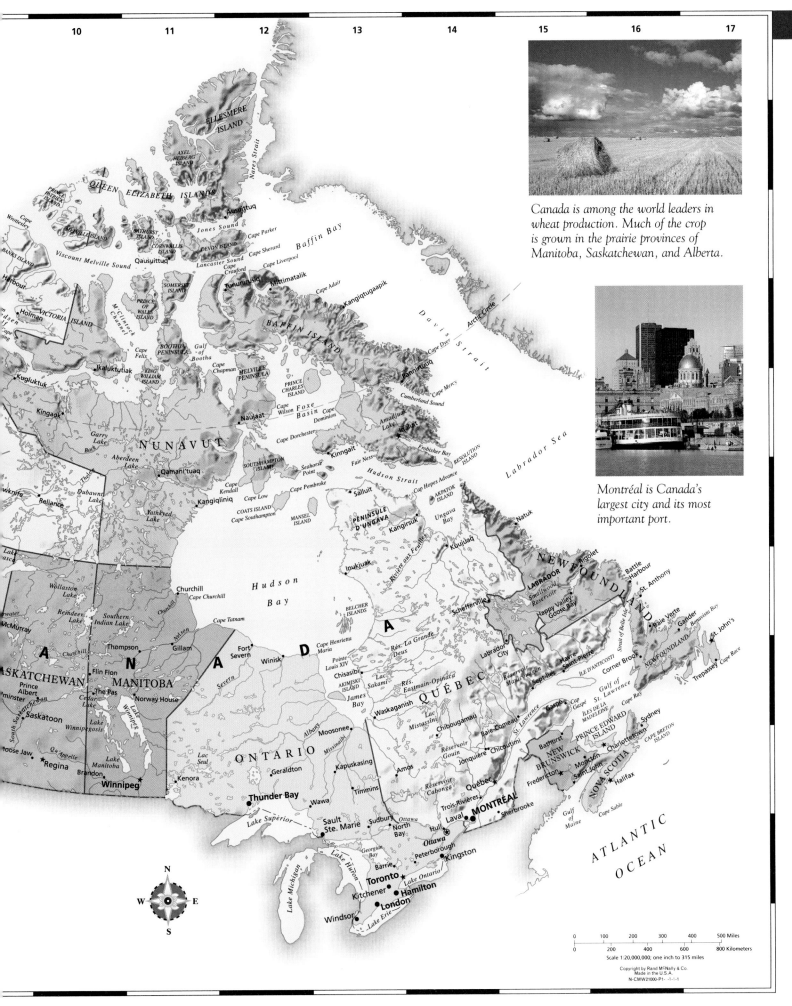

Canada is among the world leaders in wheat production. Much of the crop is grown in the prairie provinces of Manitoba, Saskatchewan, and Alberta.

Montréal is Canada's largest city and its most important port.

ELLESMERE ISLAND

AXEL HEIBERG ISLAND

QUEEN ELIZABETH ISLANDS

PRINCE PATRICK ISLAND

Cape Wrottesley

MELVILLE ISLAND

BATHURST ISLAND

CORNWALLIS ISLAND

DEVON ISLAND

Jones Sound

Cape Parker

Nares Strait

Baffin Bay

BANKS ISLAND

Viscount Melville Sound

Qausuittuq

Ausuittuq

Lancaster Sound

Cape Sherard

Cape Crawford

Cape Liverpool

Harbour

Holman

VICTORIA ISLAND

M'Clintock Channel

PRINCE OF WALES ISLAND

SOMERSET ISLAND

Tununirusiq

Mittimatalik

Cape Adair

Kangiqtugaapik

Davis Strait

Arctic Circle

Kugluktuk

Ikaluktutiak

BOOTHIA PENINSULA

Gulf of Boothia

KING WILLIAM ISLAND

Cape Felix

Cape Chapman

MELVILLE PENINSULA

BAFFIN ISLAND

Cape Dyer

Kingaok

Cape Wilson

Foxe Basin

PRINCE CHARLES ISLAND

Pannirtuuq

Cumberland Sound

Cape Mercy

Naujaat

Cape Dominion

Amadjuak Lake

Iqaluit

NUNAVUT

Garry Lake

Back

Aberdeen Lake

Cape Dorchester

SOUTHAMPTON ISLAND

Seahorse Point

Kinngait

Fair Ness

Frobisher Bay

RESOLUTION ISLAND

Labrador Sea

kwnife

Thelon

Dubawnt Lake

Reliance

Qamani'tuaq

Cape Kendall

Hudson Strait

Yathkyed Lake

Kangiqliniq

Cape Low

Cape Pembroke

COATS ISLAND

Cape Southampton

MANSEL ISLAND

Salluit

Cap Hopes Advance

AKPATOK ISLAND

Natuk

Lake asca

Wollaston Lake

Reindeer Lake

PENINSULE D'UNGAVA

Kangirsuk

Ungava Bay

McMurray

Southern Indian Lake

Rivière aux Feuilles

Kuujjuaq

NEWFOUNDLAND

Nain

Nachvak

Chandhal

Churchill

Hudson Bay

Inukjuak

LABRADOR

Battle Harbour

St. Anthony

Prince Albert

Flin Flon

Thompson

Gillam

Churchill

Cape Churchill

Smallwood Reservoir

Happy Valley-Goose Bay

Baie Verte

Gander

Bonavista Bay

SASKATCHEWAN

MANITOBA

Cedar Lake

The Pas

Cape Tatnam

Fort Severn

BELCHER ISLANDS

Schefferville

Labrador City

Corner Brook

NEWFOUNDLAND

St. John's

Cape Race

Saskatoon

Lake Winnipegosis

Norway House

Winisk

Cape Henrietta Maria

Rés. La Grande Deux

Réservoir Manicouagan

Sept-Îles

ÎLE D'ANTICOSTI

Saint-Pierre

Trepassey

minster

CANADA

Pointe Louis XIV

Chisasibi

Lac Sakami

Rés. Eastmain-Opinacá

Havre-Saint-Pierre

oose Jaw

Qu'Appelle

Lake Manitoba

AKIMISKI ISLAND

James Bay

Waskaganish

Lac Mistassini

Chibougamau

Baie-Comeau

Gaspé

Cap Gaspé

ÎLES DE LA MADELEINE

Cape Ray

Regina

Brandon

Winnipeg

Lac Seul

Albany

Moosonee

Réservoir Gouin

QUÉBEC

Amos

Chicoutimi

Jonquière

Gulf of St. Lawrence

PRINCE EDWARD ISLAND

Sydney

CAPE BRETON ISLAND

ONTARIO

Missinaibi

Kapuskasing

Réservoir Cabonga

Bathurst

NEW BRUNSWICK

Charlottetown

Geraldton

Kenora

Wawa

Timmins

Québec

Trois-Rivières

Fredericton

Moncton

NOVA SCOTIA

Thunder Bay

Lake Superior

Sault Ste. Marie

Sudbury

North Bay

Hull

Laval

MONTRÉAL

Sherbrooke

Saint John

Halifax

Georgian Bay

Lake Huron

Lake Michigan

Barrie

Ottawa

Peterborough

Kingston

Lake Ontario

Gulf of Maine

Cape Sable

ATLANTIC OCEAN

Toronto

Kitchener

Hamilton

London

Windsor

Lake Erie

N
W   E
S

0   100   200   300   400   500 Miles
0   200   400   600   800 Kilometers
Scale 1:20,000,000; one inch to 315 miles

Copyright by Rand McNally & Co.
Made in the U.S.A.
N-CMW21000-P1- -1-1-1

UNITED STATES

The United States occupies the central portion of the continent, but also includes Alaska, next to Canada's northwest corner, and Hawaii, a chain of islands in the middle of the Pacific Ocean. The United States is the most prosperous and populous country in North America. It also has the world's most ethnically diverse population. A large number of the country's people live in or near its many large cities. There are other areas, especially in the west, where the population is extremely sparse. The landscape of the United States is varied and beautiful, ranging from stark deserts and rocky canyons to majestic mountains and endless plains.

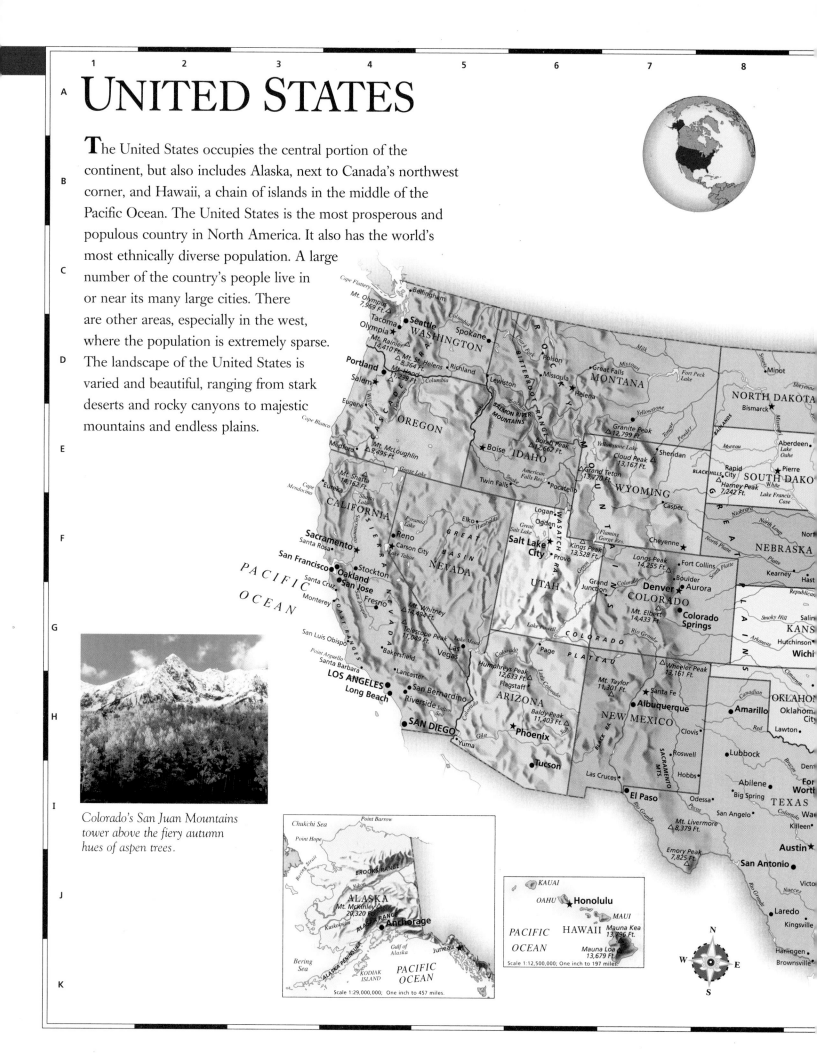

Colorado's San Juan Mountains tower above the fiery autumn hues of aspen trees.

Cape Flattery
Bellingham
Mt. Olympus 7,969 Ft.
Tacoma
Olympia
Seattle
Spokane
WASHINGTON
Columbia
Mt. Rainier 14,410 Ft.
Mt. St. Helens 8,364 Ft.
Richland
Polson
Portland
Mt. Hood 11,239 Ft.
Lewiston
Missoula
Great Falls
Missouri
MONTANA
Fort Peck Lake
Minot
Sheyenne
Salem
Columbia
Helena
NORTH DAKOTA
Bismarck
Eugene
OREGON
Yellowstone
Granite Peak 12,799 Ft.
Tongue
BADLANDS
Aberdeen Lake Oahe
Cape Blanco
SALMON RIVER MOUNTAINS
Boise
IDAHO
Borah Peak 12,662 Ft.
Yellowstone Lake
Cloud Peak 13,167 Ft.
Sheridan
Rapid City
BLACK HILLS
SOUTH DAKOTA
Pierre
Medford
Mt. McLoughlin 9,495 Ft.
Snake
Grand Teton 13,770 Ft.
WYOMING
Harney Peak 7,242 Ft.
Lake Francis Case
Mt. Shasta 14,162 Ft.
Goose Lake
Twin Falls
American Falls Res.
Pocatello
Niobrara
Cape Mendocino
Eureka
Shasta Lake
Elko
Humboldt
Logan
Ogden
Great Salt Lake
WASATCH
Flaming Gorge Res.
Casper
North Loup
North Platte
NEBRASKA
Norf
CALIFORNIA
Pyramid Lake
Reno
Carson City
Lake Tahoe
Salt Lake City
Provo
Cheyenne
Longs Peak 14,255 Ft.
Fort Collins
South Platte
Platte
Kearney
Hast
Sacramento
Santa Rosa
GREAT
BASIN
NEVADA
Green
Colorado
Boulder
Aurora
Denver
Republican
San Francisco
Oakland
Stockton
Santa Cruz
San Jose
Monterey
Fresno
San Joaquin
Grand Junction
COLORADO
Mt. Elbert 14,433 Ft.
Colorado Springs
Smoky Hill
KANS
Hutchinson
Salin
Wichi
PACIFIC
OCEAN
COAST RANGES
Mt. Whitney 14,494 Ft.
Telescope Peak 11,049 Ft.
Lake Mead
Lake Powell
COLORADO
PLATEAU
Rio Grande
Arkansas
San Luis Obispo
Point Arguello
Santa Barbara
Bakersfield
Las Vegas
Colorado
Page
Wheeler Peak 13,161 Ft.
Cimarron
OKLAHOM
Lancaster
LOS ANGELES
Long Beach
San Bernardino
Riverside
Salton Sea
Humphreys Peak 12,633 Ft.
Flagstaff
Little Colorado
Mt. Taylor 11,301 Ft.
Santa Fe
Canadian
Amarillo
Oklahoma City
SAN DIEGO
Yuma
Gila
ARIZONA
Baldy Peak 11,403 Ft.
Phoenix
NEW MEXICO
Albuquerque
Clovis
Red
Lawton
Colorado
Salt
BLACK RA.
Roswell
Lubbock
Den
Tucson
Las Cruces
SACRAMENTO MTS.
Hobbs
Abilene
Big Spring
TEXAS
For Wort
El Paso
Pecos
Odessa
San Angelo
Colorado
Wa
Killeen
Mt. Livermore 8,379 Ft.
Rio Grande
Brazos
Austin
Emory Peak 7,825 Ft.
San Antonio
Nueces
Victo
Laredo
Kingsville
Rio Grande
Harlingen
Brownsville

Alaska inset:
Chukchi Sea
Point Barrow
Point Hope
BROOKS RANGE
Bering Strait
Yukon
ALASKA
Mt. McKinley 20,320 Ft.
Kuskokwim
ALASKA RANGE
Anchorage
Juneau
Bering Sea
Kuskokwim
ALASKA PENINSULA
KODIAK ISLAND
Gulf of Alaska
PACIFIC OCEAN
Scale 1:29,000,000; One inch to 457 miles.

Hawaii inset:
KAUAI
OAHU
Honolulu
MAUI
PACIFIC OCEAN
HAWAII
Mauna Kea 13,796 Ft.
Mauna Loa 13,679 Ft.
Scale 1:12,500,000; One inch to 197 miles.

N
W E
S

The Navajo are one of many Native American tribes that live in the desert Southwest.

The design of many state capitol buildings imitates the dome shape of the U.S. Capitol in Washington, D.C.

Limestone-rich grasses in Kentucky contain a lot of calcium; horses that eat them often become strong runners.

Four surfers walk along the beach in southern California.

Prairie dogs make their homes in burrows across the central and western parts of the United States.

Scale 1:16,000,000; one inch to 252 miles.
Copyright by Rand McNally
Made in the U.S.A.
N-CMW24000-P1- -1-i-1

MEXICO, CENTRAL AMERICA, AND THE CARIBBEAN

A B C D E F G H I J K

1 2 3 4 5 6 7 8

Tijuana
Ensenada
Mexicali
BAJA CALIFORNIA
Cerro de Encantada 10,069 Ft.
Nogales
Agua Prieta
Ciudad Juárez
Rio Grande
Gulf of California
ISLA CEDROS
Punta Eugenia
SONORA
Hermosillo
Chihuahua
Ciudad Acuña
Piedras Negras
GULF OF MEXICO
Empalme
Volcan Las Tres Virgenes 6,299 Ft.
Ciudad Obregón
Chauhtémoc
Delicias
Chihuahua
Nueva Rosita
BAJA CALIFORNIA SUR
Hidalgo del Parral
Camargo
COAHUILA
Nuevo Laredo
Monclova
Los Mochis
Guasave
Guamuchil
Gómez Palacio
San Pedro de las Colonias
NUEVO LEÓN
Frontera
Reynosa
MONTERREY
Matamoros
La Paz
Tropic of Cancer
DURANGO
Torreón
Saltillo
Linares
Cabo San Lucas
SINALOA
Durango
ZACATECAS
MEXICO
TAMAULIPAS
Ciudad Victoria
Mazatlán
Matehuala
Ciudad Mante
GULF OF MEXICO
Fresnillo
SAN LUIS POTOSÍ
Zacatecas
Ciudad Madero
NAYARIT
AGUASCALIENTES
San Luis Potosí
Tampico
ISLAS MARÍAS
Tepic
Aguascalientes
Ciudad Valles
Puerto Vallarta
León
Guanajuato
Cabo Rojo
ISLAS REVILLAGIGEDO
ISLA SAN BENEDICTO
Tepatitlán
GUANAJUATO
Querétaro
Tuxpan
Poza Rica
Mérida
ISLA ROCA PARTIDA
GUADALAJARA
JALISCO
Irapuato
QUERÉTARO
Pachuca
Martínez de la Torre
YUCATÁN
Cancún
ISLA SOCORRO
Ciudad Guzmán
Morelia
HIDALGO
VERACRUZ
Campeche
YUCATÁN PENINSULA
Colima
Uruapan
MEXICO CITY
Xalapa
QUINTANA ROO
COLIMA
Tecomán
MICHOACÁN
MEXICO
TLAXCALA
Pico de Orizaba 18,406 Ft.
Córdoba
Bahía de Campeche
Roadrunner
Toluca
Cuernavaca
Puebla
Orizaba
Veracruz
CAMPECHE
Chetumal
MORELOS
PUEBLA
Tehuacán
Coatzacoalcos
TABASCO
Ciudad del Carmen
GUERRERO
Chilpancingo
Minatlán
Villahermosa
Belize City
Acapulco
OAXACA
Oaxaca
Belmopan
BELIZE
ISLA ROAT
SIERRA MADRE DEL SUR
Tuxtla Gutiérrez
San Cristóbal de las Casas
Gulf of Honduras
Juchitán
CHIAPAS
Venustiano Carranza
San Ped Sula
Golfo de Tehuantepec
Volcan Tajumulco 13,845 Ft.
GUATEMALA
El Progre
HONDUR
Tapachula
GUATEMALA
Tegucig
PACIFIC OCEAN
Quezaltenango
Santa Ana
Escuintla
Sonsonate
Cojutepeque
San Miguel
Choluteca
San Salvador
San Vicente
Chinandega
EL SALVADOR
León
Managua
Nica
Cabo Sante

Roadrunner

Mexico, settled by Spaniards, has the largest Spanish-speaking population in the world. Most Mexicans live in cities—one-fourth of them in Mexico City alone. Mexico has large oil fields and silver deposits in its arid northern and western regions, and lush rain forests in the south, near the mountainous and densely forested countries of Central America. The "Mosquito Coast," along the Caribbean shore of Honduras, Nicaragua, and Costa Rica, is a sparsely populated land of swamps and abundant wildlife. Elsewhere in Central America, agriculture, especially coffee, beans, and bananas, is an important part of the economy. To the east of Mexico and Central America in the Caribbean Sea lie hundreds of coral and volcanic islands, inhabited by a vibrant mix of Africans, Asians, and Europeans. Many Caribbean islands are still controlled by the European countries that settled them centuries ago. The islands' coral-sand beaches and turquoise waters attract many tourists and cruise ships.

A bustling outdoor market in Guadalajara, Mexico, sells fruit, clothing, and toys.

10   11   12   13   14   15   16   17

A tugboat guides a tanker through the Panama Canal.

In Cuba, dominos is a common pasttime.

ATLANTIC

OCEAN

GRAND
BAHAMA

ABACO

BAHAMAS
Nassau
NEW
PROVIDENCE   ELEUTHERA
CAT ISLAND

ANDROS

Straits of Florida   LONG ISLAND

Tropic of Cancer

MAYAGUANA

ACKLINS

TURKS AND CAICOS ISLANDS
(U.K.)

HAVANA   Matanzas
Artemisa   Cárdenas
Güines   Placetas
Santa Clara
Pinar del Rio   Morón
Cienfuegos   Florida
Trinidad
ISLA DE LA   Camagüey   Holguín   Banes
JUVENTUD
CUBA
Manzanillo   Bayamo

GREAT
INAGUA   CAICOS
ISLANDS   Grand Turk

W   E   S   T

I   N   D   I   E   S

Puerto
Plata
Guantánamo   Santiago
Cap-Haïtien   San Francisco de Macoris   **VIRGIN   BRITISH
ISLANDS   VIRGIN
(U.S.)   ISLANDS**   ANGUILLA
(U.K.)
CAYMAN ISLANDS   Cabo   Santiago   Gonaïves   **SANTO DOMINGO**   San Juan   ANTIGUA
(U.K.)   Cruz   de Cuba   **HAITI**   La Romana   San Juan   Ponce   ST. CROIX   AND
George Town   Barahona   Mayagüez   BARBUDA
Montego Bay   **Port-au-Prince**   **PUERTO RICO**   St. John's
HISPANIOLA   (U.S.)   ST. KITTS AND NEVIS
Spanish Town   **DOMINICAN
Kingston   REPUBLIC**   MONTSERRAT   Pointe-à-Pitre
JAMAICA   (U.K.)   **GUADELOUPE**
Basse-Terre   (Fr.)
DOMINICA   Roseau
Fort-de-France
MARTINIQUE
Cabo   (Fr.)
Camarón   Castries   **ST. LUCIA**
Cabo de Gracias a Dios   **CARIBBEAN   SEA**   BARBADOS
ST. VINCENT   Bridgetown
AND THE
GRENADINES   Kingstown
GRENADA
St. George's

G   R   E   A   T   E   R

A   N   T   I   L   L   E   S

L   E   S   S   E   R

A   N   T   I   L   L   E   S

ARUBA
(Neth.)   **NETHERLANDS
ANTILLES**
Oranjestad   CURAÇAO   BONAIRE
Willemstad   Port of Spain
TRINIDAD AND TOBAGO
TRINIDAD
San Fernando

TOBAGO

NICARAGUA

San José
Volcán Irazú   Puerto Limón
11,260 Ft.   Cerro Chirripó   Golfo de los   Colón
△12,530 Ft.   Mosquitos
COSTA RICA   **PANAMÁ**
Volcán Barú   La Chorrera   ISTMO
11,491 Ft.   David   DE   PANAMÁ
Punta Burica   Golfo de   ISLA
Chiriquí   DEL REY
**PENÍNSULA
DE AZUERO**   Golfo
ISLA DE COIBA   de
Panamá   Punta Mala
Punta Mariato   **PANAMA**

0   100   200   300   400   500 Miles
0   200   400   600   800 Kilometers
Scale 1:16,000,000; one inch to 252 miles
Copyright by Rand McNally & Co.
Made in U.S.A.
N-CMW30000-P1- -5-1-1

Tropical rain forests blanket much of Costa Rica.

Cabo San Lucas, at the southern tip of Mexico's Baja Peninsula, is known for its stunning rock arches.

SOUTH AMERICA

The architecture of Peru's Machu Picchu (above) reflects an advanced Inca culture; lush rain forests (below) cover Venezuela's Bolívar state; the toucan (right) lives in the rain forests of South America.

South America is a continent of geographical extremes, known for its tropical rain forests as well as the driest desert on Earth–the cold, desolate Atacama Desert in Chile. South America's northern border lies north of the equator on the Caribbean Sea. Its southernmost point at Cape Horn is only 600 miles (970 kilometers) from Antarctica. The Andes, which stretch along the entire western edge of the continent, form the longest mountain chain in the world. The highest peaks of the Andes are surpassed in height only by the Himalayas in Asia.

South America also boasts the world's largest river basin, the Amazon Basin; the world's highest waterfall, Angel Falls in Venezuela; and the world's highest lake used for transportation, Lake Titicaca on the border of Peru and Bolivia. Other principal landscape features include the broad plains of Bolivia and Paraguay's Gran Chaco and Argentina's Pampa, and the arid, rocky tablelands of Patagonia.

South America Facts

Area: 6,900,000 square miles (17,800,000 square kilometers)

Highest Mountain: Cerro Aconcagua, Argentina, 22,831 feet (6,959 meters)

Lowest Point: Salinas Chicas, Argentina, -138 feet (-42 meters)

Longest River: Amazon, 4,000 miles (6,400 kilometers)

Largest Lake: Lake Titicaca, Peru-Bolivia, 3,200 square miles (8,300 square kilometers)

Largest Desert: Atacama Desert, Chile, 57,000 square miles (148,000 square kilometers)

Largest Island: Tierra del Fuego, Chile-Argentina, 18,600 square miles (48,200 square kilometers)

Highest Waterfall: Angel Falls, Venezuela, 3,212 feet (979 meters)—*world's highest waterfall*

CARIBBEAN SEA

ATLANTIC
OCEAN

Punta
Gallinas
Pico Cristóbal Colón
18,947 Ft.
CARACAS
Boca Grande
Punta
Magdalena
Lago de
Maracaibo
Orinoco
Golfo
de
Panamá
Llanos
VENEZUELA
GUYANA
SURINAME
FRENCH
GUIANA
Cabo Orange
Pakaraima Mts.
Nev. del Tolima
17,110 Ft.
BOGOTÁ
COLOMBIA
Nev. del Huila
18,865 Ft.

Equator
Punta Galera
Equator
ECUADOR
Chimborazo
20,702 Ft.
Putumayo
Japurá
Negro
MANAUS
Amazon
ILHA DE
MARAJÓ
Belém

GALAPAGOS
ISLANDS
Amazon
Amazon
Basin
Juruá
Madeira
Tapajós
Tocantins
B R A Z I L
Cabo de
São Roque
Punta Pariñas
Selvas
Uruaíl
Represa de
Sobradinho
RECIFE

A
n
d
e
s
Nev. Huascarán
22,133 Ft.
PERU
Planalto do
Mato Grosso
LIMA
Nev. Illampu
21,066 Ft.
Lago Titicaca
BOLIVIA
BRASÍLIA
Ponta da Baleia
Punta Carreta
Cordillera Real
Nev. Sajama
21,463 Ft.
São Francisco
Serra do Espinhaço

PACIFIC
OCEAN

Tropic of Capricorn
Gran Chaco
PARAGUAY
Paraná
Cabo de São Tomé
Tropic of Capricorn
ISLA SAN AMBROSIO
Atacama Desert
Nev. Ojos del Salado
22,615 Ft.
SÃO PAULO
RIO DE
JANEIRO
ISLA SAN FELIX
Paraná
Lagoa dos
Patos
ARCHIPIÉLAGO
JUAN FERNÁNDEZ
C
H
I
L
E
A
n
d
e
s
A
R
G
E
N
T
I
N
A
Pampa
Paraná
Cerro
Aconcagua
22,831 Ft.
Santiago
URUGUAY
Lagoa Mirim
BUENOS
AIRES
Río de la Plata

ATLANTIC
OCEAN

Punta Lavapié
Golfo San Matías
Peninsula Valdés
Cabo Quedal
ISLA GRANDE
DE CHILOÉ
ARCHIPIÉLAGO DE
LOS CHONOS
Cabo dos Bahías
Golfo San Jorge
Peninsula
de Taito
Punta Medanoso
ISLA
WELLINGTON
FALKLAND ISLANDS
(U.K.)
Bahía
Grande
WEST
FALKLAND
EAST
FALKLAND
Strait of Magellan
ISLA DESOLACIÓN
TIERRA DEL
FUEGO
ISLA SANTA
INÉS
Cape Horn

Land Elevation
Feet (Meters)

9,840 and over (3,000 and over)
6,560 - 9,840 (2,000 - 3,000)
3,280 - 6,560 (1,000 - 2,000)
1,640 - 3,280 (500 - 1,000)
656 - 1,640 (200 - 500)
0 - 656 feet (0 - 200)

N
W   E
S

0 100 200 300 400 500 Miles
0 200 400 600 800 Kilometers
Scale 1:45,000,000; one inch to 710 miles

Copyright by Rand McNally & Co. Made in U.S.A.
N-CMW40000-A1- -1- -1

THE LAND

South America is known for its plentiful animal and plant life, most of which is found in the wilderness that covers a large part of the continent, from the jagged peaks of the Andes to the thick jungles of the Amazon Basin. Only about seven percent of the land is naturally suited for farming. South America is rich in mineral resources, but its industries are not well developed; most raw materials are exported and manufactured into products outside of the continent.

Brazil is one of the world's leading exporters of bananas.

Economies

- Little or no activity
- Nomadic herding
- Hunting, forestry, subsistence farming
- Forestry
- Agriculture
- Stock raising
- Manufacturing, commerce
- Fishing

© Rand McNally

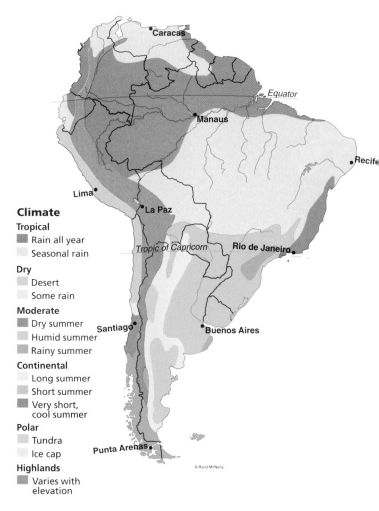

Climate

Tropical
- Rain all year
- Seasonal rain

Dry
- Desert
- Some rain

Moderate
- Dry summer
- Humid summer
- Rainy summer

Continental
- Long summer
- Short summer
- Very short, cool summer

Polar
- Tundra
- Ice cap

Highlands
- Varies with elevation

© Rand McNally

Economies

Stock raising, agriculture, and subsistence farming are important to South America's economy. Many parts of the rain forest have been burned out and cleared for farming, livestock grazing, and development. These slash-and-burn tactics have destroyed more than 200,000 square miles (518,000 square kilometers) of the Amazon rain forest in just 20 years. More than 40 square miles (103 square kilometers) vanish each day.

Climate

Tropical rain forest climates–hot and wet–and tropical savanna climates–hot with rainy and dry seasons–prevail in northern South America. Climates in the southern portion of the continent range from temperate, or moderate, to the subarctic chill of Tierra del Fuego. In parts of South America, the Andes block moist Pacific Ocean breezes from moving east, creating dry weather in the Patagonia region east of the mountains in Argentina and Chile. In other areas, the Andes rise alongside tropical regions.

Farming and Ranching

Many South Americans are involved in farming; some are subsistence farmers who grow only enough corn, beans, and potatoes to feed their families, while others work on huge commercial farms that produce crops for export. Cocoa, coffee, sugarcane, and bananas grow in abundance. Since much of the continent lies in the Southern Hemisphere—where the seasons are opposite those in the Northern Hemisphere—some countries export oranges, lemons, and grapes to the north during the northern winter. Vast cattle ranches dot the Gran Chaco of Bolivia and Paraguay, the Pampa of Argentina, and the Llanos of Venezuela and Colombia, while sheep graze the windswept landscapes of Patagonia and Tierra del Fuego.

Environments

- Forest
- Swamp
- Crop and woodland
- Cropland
- Crop and grazing land
- Grassland
- Desert
- Tundra
- Barren
- Urban

© Rand McNally

Trekkers marvel at the beauty of Peru's snow-covered Andes.

Mining and Mineral Resources

Gold and silver, which drew Europeans to South America more than 500 years ago, are now mined in much smaller quantities than they once were. More than one-quarter of Earth's copper is buried in the Andes, where Chile's Chuquicamata, the world's most expansive open-pit mine, lies over the largest known copper deposit. Iron, bauxite, manganese, zinc, lead, oil, and natural gas are among the continent's important mineral resources.

Industry

While many of South America's industries remain underdeveloped, the more industrialized countries manufacture and process food, metals, chemicals, petroleum, textiles, clothing, cars, and appliances. Brazil is by far the leading industrial and economic producer on the continent, with Argentina, Venezuela, and Chile also contributing to the industrial sector.

Hundreds of oil rigs rise from the waters of Venezuela's Lake Maracaibo.

The Itaipu Dam on the Paraña River between Brazil and Paraguay provides hydroelectric power.

Tourism

Although tourism to cities such as Rio de Janeiro, Brazil, and Caracas, Venezuela, has declined in recent years, growing interest in adventure and nature-oriented travel is turning South America's more remote regions into prime vacation destinations. Travelers flock to study wildlife on the Galapagos Islands, experience history atop moss-covered Inca ruins high in the Andes, float down the Amazon, and trek through the starkly beautiful landscapes of Patagonia.

THE PEOPLE

Three girls in Peru wear the traditional clothing of the Quechua people.

The panpipe creates a distinctive sound in Ecuadorian music.

Rio de Janeiro celebrates Carnival every year with lavish costumes, music, and dancing.

South America's rich heritage comes from a vibrant combination of American Indian, European, and African peoples. From the sixteenth to the nineteenth centuries, Spain and Portugal controlled most of South America; today Spanish and Portuguese are the most widely spoken languages on the continent. Most South Americans live in crowded coastal cities–ninety percent of the population resides within 150 miles (240 kilometers) of the ocean. Native peoples, however, still dwell deep in the rain forests and the rugged high country. In the second half of the twentieth century, people from around the world immigrated to South America in search of new opportunities in trade and agriculture. Substantial Asian populations live in Brazil, Argentina, and Peru, for example. One of South America's most pressing social problems is the unequal distribution of wealth: A small percentage of rich people control most of the property, while great numbers of poor people crowd into makeshift shanty towns and squatter settlements called *favelas* that lie on the outskirts of the major cities.

Musicians serenade passers-by outside cafes and restaurants.

A Bolivian woman carries her baby on her back.

Two boys ride horses in Paraguay.

CARIBBEAN SEA

ATLANTIC

OCEAN

Punta
Gallinas
Barranquilla **MARACAIBO** *CARACAS*
Cartagena Cúcuta **Barquisimeto** Boca Grande
Orinoco Georgetown
MEDELLÍN Bucaramanga **VENEZUELA** Paramaribo
Nev. del Tolima Llanos **GUYANA** Cayenne
17,110 Ft. *BOGOTÁ* **SURINAME** **FRENCH**
Punta Magdalena **COLOMBIA** **GUIANA**
CALI Boa Vista Cabo Caciporé
Nev. del Huila Macapá Cabo Norte
18,865 Ft.
Punta Galera Lérida *ILHA DE* *Baía de Marajó* Equator
Equator **QUITO** MARAJÓ
Cayambe Japurá **MANAUS** *Amazon* **Belém** São Luis
ECUADOR 18,996 Ft. Putumayo Negro
GUAYAQUIL Tefé Santarém **Fortaleza**
Iquitos Amazon Tocantins Imperatriz **Teresina** Cabo de São Roque
Punta Pariñas Juruá Madeira Tapajós **B R A Z I L** Conceição do **Natal**
Chiclayo Araguaia
Ji-Parana Represa de
Nev. Huascarán Ucayali Planalto do Sobradinho São Francisco **RECIFE**
22,133 Ft. Mato Grosso Feira **Aracaju**
Callao Cuzco Puerto Heath de Santana
Punta Carreta **LIMA** *Nev. Illampu* Cuiabá **SALVADOR**
Lago 21,066 Ft. Goiânia Itabuna
Titicaca **LA PAZ** **BRASÍLIA**
Arequipa **BOLIVIA** Uberlândia Ponta da Baleia
Oruro Santa Cruz Represa de
PACIFIC Sucre de la Sierra **Campo** Três Marias
Nev. Sajama **Grande**
OCEAN 21,463 Ft. **BELO HORIZONTE**
Iquique Grán Chaco Londrina Cabo de São Tomé
Tropic of Capricorn **PARAGUAY** **SÃO** **RIO DE JANEIRO**
Antofagasta Paraná **PAULO** Santo André
Punta Ballenita *Asunción* Florianópolis
ISLA SAN AMBROSIO *Nev. Ojos del Salado* **San Miguel** Santa
(Chile) 22,615 Ft. **de Tucumán** Maria
Punta Cachos Goya Lagoa dos **PORTO ALEGRE**
ISLA SAN FÉLIX Paraná Patos
(Chile) **CÓRDOBA** Santa Fe Lagoa Mirim
Valparaíso Cerro **ROSARIO** **URUGUAY**
ARCHIPIÉLAGO Aconcagua **BUENOS** **MONTEVIDEO**
JUAN FERNÁNDEZ 22,831 Ft. **AIRES** Punta del Este
(Chile) **Santiago** **La Plata** Río de la Plata
Concepción *ATLANTIC*
Punta Lavapié *Pampa* Bahía
Valdivia Neuquén Blanca **Mar del Plata** *OCEAN*
Cabo Quedal
Golfo San Matias
ISLA GRANDE DE CHILOÉ **Península Valdés**
ARCHIPIÉLAGO DE LOS CHONOS Cabo dos Bahías
Golfo San Jorge
Península Comodoro Rivadavia
de Taitao Punta Medanoso

FALKLAND ISLANDS
ISLA WELLINGTON Bahía **(U.K.)**
Grande WEST
FALKLAND
Strait of Magellan *Stanley*
Punta Arenas TIERRA DEL EAST FALKLAND
FUEGO
ISLA SANTA INÉS Cape Horn

N
W E
S

0 100 200 300 400 500 Miles
0 200 400 600 800 Kilometers
Scale 1:45,000,000; one inch to 710 miles
Copyright by Rand McNally & Co. Made in U.S.A.
N-CMW40000-P1- -1-1-1

South America Facts

Population:
340,000,000

Population Density:
49 people per square mile
(19 per square kilometer)

Most Populous Country:
Brazil, 170,860,000 people

Largest City:
São Paulo, Brazil,
17,200,000 people
(metropolitan area)

A Brazilian boy holds his pet dog.

NORTHERN SOUTH AMERICA

Mountains and rain forests dominate the northern portion of South America. Besides the Andes, other highland areas rise in Guiana and Brazil, which lie north and south of the Amazon Basin, respectively. The tropical rain forests that fill the basins of the Amazon and Orinoco Rivers provide a home for more than 1,500 species of fish, 8,000 species of insects, and 1.6 million species of plants. In the Andes, many remnants of Inca culture, including the impressive ruins at Machu Picchu, have survived for centuries.

Tapirs are strong swimmers, but they can also move quickly through their jungle habitats.

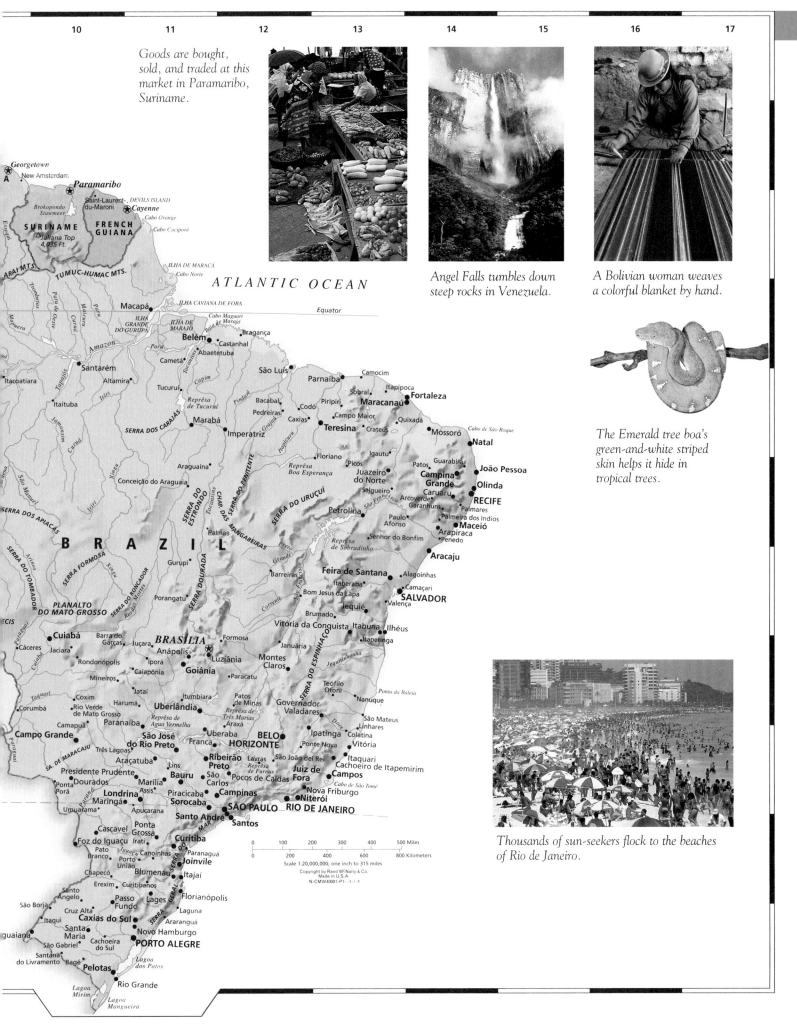

Goods are bought, sold, and traded at this market in Paramaribo, Suriname.

Angel Falls tumbles down steep rocks in Venezuela.

A Bolivian woman weaves a colorful blanket by hand.

The Emerald tree boa's green-and-white striped skin helps it hide in tropical trees.

Thousands of sun-seekers flock to the beaches of Rio de Janeiro.

ATLANTIC OCEAN

Equator

Georgetown
New Amsterdam
Paramaribo
Saint-Laurent-   DEVILS ISLAND
du-Maroni   **Cayenne**
Cabo Orange
Brokopondo   Cabo Caciporé
Stuwmeer
SURINAME   **FRENCH**
△ Juliana Top   **GUIANA**
4,035 Ft.
ARAI MTS.
TUMUC-HUMAC MTS.
ILHA DE MARACÁ
Cabo Norte
ILHA CAVIANA DE FORA

Macapá
Cabo Maguari
ILHA   Baía de Marajó
GRANDE   ILHA DE
DO GURUPÁ   MARAJÓ
Amazon   Bragança
Pará   **Belém**
Santarém   Cametá   Castanhal
Altamira   Abaetetuba
São Luís   Camocim
Itacoatiara   Tucuruí   Parnaíba   Itapipoca
Itaituba   Represa   Bacabal   Sobral   Fortaleza
de Tucuruí   Codó   Piripiri   Campo Maior   **Maracanaú**
Pedreiras   Caxias   Mossoró
Marabá   Crateús   **Natal**
Imperatriz   **Teresina**   Quixadá   Cabo de São Roque
Floriano   Igatu
Araguaína   Picos   Guarabira
Represa   Juazeiro   Patos   **João Pessoa**
Conceição do Araguaia   Boa Esperança   do Norte   **Campina**   **Olinda**
Salgueiro   **Grande**   Caruaru   **RECIFE**
Arcoverde   Garanhuns   Palmares
Palmas   Petrolina   Paulo   Palmeira dos Indios
Gurupi   Afonso   **Maceió**
B R A Z I L   Arapiraca
Represa   Senhor do Bonfim   Penedo
de Sobradinho
SERRA DOS APIACAS   Barreiras   **Aracaju**
SERRA FORMOSA   Feira de Santana   Alagoinhas
SERRA DO TOMBADOR   Bom Jesus da Lapa   Camaçari
PLANALTO   Itaberaba   **SALVADOR**
CECIS   **DO MATO GROSSO**   Porangatu   Jequié   Valença
Brumado
Cuiabá   Barra do   Vitória da Conquista   Itabuna   Ilhéus
Cáceres   Garças   Formosa   Itapetinga
Jaciara   **BRASÍLIA**   Januária
Rondonópolis   Anápolis   Montes   SERRA DO ESPINHAÇO
Iporá   Luziânia   Claros   Jequitinhonha
Mineiros   Caiapônia   **Goiânia**   Paracatu   Teófilo
Jataí   Itumbiara   Otoni   Ponta da Baleia
Coxim   Harumá   Patos   Nanúque
Corumbá   Rio Verde   de Minas   **Uberlândia**   Governador   São Mateus
de Mato Grosso   Represa de   Valadares   Linhares
Camapuã   Araxá   Represa de   Ipatinga   Colatina
Campo Grande   **Paranaíba**   Três Marias   **BELO**   Ponte Nova   Vitória
Uberaba   **HORIZONTE**   Itaquari
SA. DE MARACAJU   **São José**   Franca   São João del Rei   Cachoeiro de Itapemirim
Três Lagoas   **do Rio Preto**   **Ribeirão**   Lavras   Cabo de São Tomé
Araçatuba   **Preto**   Represa   Juiz de   **Campos**
Presidente Prudente   Lins   São   de Furnas   **Fora**
Dourados   **Bauru**   Carlos   Poços de Caldas   Nova Friburgo
Ponta   Marília   Assis   Piracicaba   **Campinas**   **Niterói**
Porã   Apucarana   **Sorocaba**   **SÃO PAULO**   **RIO DE JANEIRO**
Londrina   **Santo André**   **Santos**
Umuarama   **Maringá**   Ponta
Cascavel   Grossa
Foz do Iguaçu   Irati   **Curitiba**
Pato   Canoinhas   Paranaguá
Branco   Porto   Joinvile
Chapecó   União   Itajaí
Erexim   Curitibanos   Blumenau
Santo   Lages   Florianópolis
Ângelo   Passo
São Borja   Fundo   Laguna
Cruz Alta   Araranguá
Itaqui   **Caxias do Sul**
Santa   Novo Hamburgo
guaiana   Maria   **PORTO ALEGRE**
São Gabriel   Cachoeira
Santana   do Sul   Lagoa
do Livramento   Bagé   **Pelotas**   dos Patos
Rio Grande
Lagoa
Mirim   Lagoa
Mangueira

0   100   200   300   400   500 Miles
0   200   400   600   800 Kilometers
Scale 1:20,000,000; one inch to 315 miles
Copyright by Rand McNally & Co.
Made in U.S.A.
N-CMW40091-P1- -1-1-1

SOUTHERN SOUTH AMERICA

Southern South America is shaped like a long cone. The Andes span the western side of this region, separating Chile from Argentina. The landscape includes the Atacama Desert to the west of the Andes, grasslands and dry tablelands to the east, and glaciers and fjords at the southernmost tip of the continent. Spanish is the main language here, but a few native groups continue to speak their own languages.

Grapes are grown in Chile and Argentina for food and for making wine.

Los Cuernos, a series of sculpted peaks, is one of the most spectacular sights in the southern Andes.

Asunción, Paraguay's capital city, still retains its Spanish colonial character.

Tango, the music and dance of Argentina, began in the slums of Buenos Aires.

Gauchos, or cowboys, have lived on the Pampa plains of Argentina for 300 years. They work on ranches and ride Criollos, a breed of wild horse.

1 2 3 4 5 6 7

A
B
C
D
E
F
G
H
I
J
K

PACIFIC

OCEAN

ATLANTIC

OCEAN

CORDILLERA OCCIDENTAL

Iquique

ATACAMA DESERT

Calama

CORDILLERA DOMEYKO

Cerro Licancábur
19,409 Ft.

Tropic of Capricorn

Volcán
Llullaillaco
22,110 Ft.

Antofagasta

Cerro Galán
19,396 Ft.

Punta Ballenita

Nevado Ojos
del Salado
22,615 Ft.

Punta Cachos

Copiapó

Cerro Bonete
22,546 Ft.

Vallenar

Punta Lengua de Vaca

La Serena

Cerro de
las Tórtolas
20,735 Ft.

Ovalle

San Juan

Cerro
Aconcagua
22,831 Ft.

SAN LUIS

Valparaíso
Quillota
Santiago
Mendoza

San Antonio
Rancagua

Mercedes

Curicó

San Rafael

Talca

Atuel

Cerro el Nevado
12,500 Ft.

Talcahuano
Concepción

Chillán

Punta Lavapié

Los Ángeles

Colorado

Temuco

Neuquén

General
Roca

Valdivia

Osorno

Cabo Quedal

Puerto Montt

San Carlos de Bariloche

Monte Tronador
11,453 Ft.

ISLA GRANDE DE CHILOÉ

Golfo Corcovado

Volcán
Corcovado
7,546 Ft.

ISLA MAGDALENA

ARCHIPIÉLAGO DE LOS CHONOS

Lago Colhué Huapí

Coihaique

Lago
Buenos Aires

PENÍNSULA DE TAITO

Golfo de Penas

Cerro
San Clemente
13,314 Ft.

ISLA CAMPANA

Cerro Chaltel
10,958 Ft.
Monte Fitzroy

ISLA WELLINGTON

Lago
Viedma

ISLA MADRE DE DIOS

Lago
Argentino

Santa Cruz

Bahía Grande

ISLA DIEGO DE ALMAGRO

Río Gallegos

ISLA DESOLACIÓN

ISLA RIESCO

Punta Arenas

TIERRA DEL FUEGO

Estrecho de Magallanes

ISLA SANTA INÉS

Ushuaia

ISLA NAVARINO

ISLA DE LOS ESTADOS

ISLA HOSTE

Cape
Horn

Estrecho de le Maire

Puerto Bahía
Negra

CHACO BOREAL

PARAGUAY

Tartagal

San Salvador
de Jujuy

Salta

Concepción

Montelindo

Pedro Juan
Caballero

Asunción

Formosa

Fernando
de la Mora

Presidencia
Roque
Sáenz Peña

Itaipú Reservoir

San Miguel
de Tucumán

Santiago
del Estero

Resistencia

Corrientes

Encarnación

Posadas

San Fernando del
Valle de Catamarca

Reconquista

Goya

La Rioja

CÓRDOBA

Laguna
Mar Chiquita

Rafaela

San
Francisco

Santa
Fe

Artigas

Concordia

Salto

Rivera

COXILHA DE SANTANA

Paraná

URUGUAY

Melo

Laguna Merín

Villa María

Río Tercero

San
Lorenzo

Paysandú

Durazno

Treinta y Tres

SAN LUIS

Río Cuarto

ROSARIO

Mercedes

Venado Tuerto

Pergamino

Zárate

San José
de Mayo

Minas

Junín

BUENOS AIRES

La
Plata

Punta del Este

MONTEVIDEO

Río de la Plata

Nueve de Julio

ARGENTINA

Santa
Rosa

Olavarría

Azul

Tandil

Salado

Tres Arroyos

Mar del Plata

Bahía Blanca

Punta Alta

Necochea

Bahía Blanca

Colorado

Negro

Viedma

Punta Rasa

Golfo
San Matías

PENÍNSULA VALDÉS

Trelew

Golfo Nuevo

Chubut

Chico

Cabo dos Bahías

Golfo San Jorge

Comodoro
Rivadavia

Deseado

Punta Medanosa

Chico

Chico

Coig

A N D E S

C H I L E

P A T A G O N I A

P A M P A

A N D E S

G R A N   C H A C O

FALKLAND ISLANDS
(U.K.)

Mount Usborne
2,312 Ft.

WEST FALKLAND

Stanley

EAST FALKLAND

Falkland Sound

0 100 200 300 400 500 Miles
0 200 400 600 800 Kilometers
Scale 1:20,000,000; one inch to 315 miles

Llamas are used for carrying goods up and down the steep slopes of the Andes.

In southern Uruguay, the town of Colonia del Sacramento borders the wide river called Rio de la Plata.

EUROPE

Europe is the second-smallest continent, but it shares the same landmass with another continent, Asia. Together, they are sometimes referred to as Eurasia.

The rounded mountains, deep fjords, and fertile plains of northern Europe were shaped by the glaciers that plowed across the region during past ice ages. Picturesque uplands and rugged mountains dominate the southern part of the continent. But the Alps in central Europe are the continent's most outstanding physical feature. These mountains began forming more than 60 million years ago when geologic forces pushed Africa northward toward Europe. The Great Northern European Plain arcs from the Pyrenees to the Urals, where Asia begins.

Switzerland's Matterhorn (above) is one of the highest peaks in the Alps; St. Basil's Cathedral (below) in Moscow, Russia, dates back to the 15th century; the scenic town of Cochem lies along the Mosel River in western Germany (below right).

ATLANTIC OCEAN

Horn
Reykjavik ICELAND
Reykjanes
Pontur
△ Hvannadalshnukur 6,952 Ft.

FAROE ISLANDS (Den.)

HEBRIDES
ORKNEY ISLANDS
SHETLAND ISLANDS
Moray Firth
Kinnaird Head
Grampian Mts.
UNITED
Firth of Forth
NORTH
KINGDOM
IRELAND
Irish Sea
Cheviot Hills
Mizen Head
St. George's Channel
GREAT BRITAIN
Thames
LONDON
NETHE- LAND
Land's End
English Channel
Strait of Dover
BELGIU
CHANNEL IS.
PARIS
Paris Basin
Loire
Seine
FRANCE
Bay of Biscay
Cabo de Fisterra
Cordillera Cantabrica
Dordogne
Massif Central
Mt. Blanc 15,771 Ft.
JU
Duero
Pyrenees
MONAC
Duero
ANDORRA
Golfe du Lion
PORTUGAL
Tagus
Iberian Peninsula
SPAIN
Sistema Iberico
Ebro
Lisbon
Cabo de São Vicente
Sierra Morena
BALEARIC ISLANDS
MENORCA
EIVISSA
MALLORCA
Strait of Gibraltar
Cap de la Nau
△ Mulhacen 11,424 Ft.
GIBRALTAR (U.K.)

N
W · E
S

Nordkapp

Murmansk

Kol'skiy poluostrov

Ponoy

Mezen'

Pechora

Ural Mountains

RWEGIAN SEA

Arctic Circle

Kebnekaise 6,926 Ft.

Lapland

White Sea

Severnaya Dvina

Onega

Kamskoye vdkhr.

Scandinavian Peninsula

Torneälven

Luleälven

FINLAND

Umeälven

Northern Uvals

Sukhona

Kama

NORWAY

SWEDEN

Galdhøpiggen 8,100 Ft.

Gulf of Bothnia

Onezhskoye ozero

Gor'kovskoye vodokhranilishche

RUSSIA

Klarälven

ÅLAND

Ladozhskoye ozero

Rybinskoye vodokhranilishche

Kuybyshevskoye vodokhranilishche

Dalälven

Stockholm

Gulf of Finland

Vänern

Vättern

GOTLAND

ESTONIA

Chudskoye ozero

Valdai Hills

MOSCOW

Oka

DENMARK

ÖLAND

Gulf of Riga

Riga

LATVIA

BALTIC SEA

SAAREMAA

Copenhagen

BORNHOLM (DEN.)

LITHUANIA

Klyaz'ma

Volga Hills

Volgogradskoye vdkhr.

Elbe

Great Northern European Plain

RUSSIA

Neman

MINSK

Central Russian Upland

Don

Tsimlyanskoye vodokhranilishche

Volga

BERLIN

Oder

POLAND

WARSAW

BELARUS

Pripyat

GERMANY

Wisła

KIEV

Dnieper Lowland

Donets Basin

Ore Mts.

Sudetes

Dniester

Dnieper

UKRAINE

CASPIAN SEA

Bohemian Forest

CZECH REPUBLIC

Carpathian Mountains

Lake Constance

SLOVAKIA

LIECH

AUSTRIA

Grossglockner 12,461 Ft.

HUNGARY

Great Hungarian Plain

MOLDOVA

Sea of Azov

ERLAND

ALPS

Danube

SLOVENIA

Drava

ROMANIA

Carpaţii Meridionali

Crimean Peninsula

gora El'brus 18,510 Ft.

Caucasus

Po

CROATIA

BLACK SEA

SAN MARINO

Apennines

BOSNIA AND HERZEGOVINA

YUGOSLAVIA

Danube

Dinaric Alps

Balkan Peninsula

ADRIATIC SEA

BULGARIA

ROME

ITALY

Vesuvius 4,190 Ft.

MACEDONIA

ALBANIA

Rhodope Mts.

Pindhos Oros

TYRRHENIAN SEA

Mt. Etna 10,902 Ft.

SICILY

Capo Passero

IONIAN SEA

GREECE

Mt. Olimbos 9,570 Ft.

Athens

AEGEAN SEA

MALTA

MEDITERRANEAN SEA

CRETE

RÓDHOS

Scale 1:16,000,000; one inch to 252 miles
Copyright by Rand McNally & Co.
Made in U.S.A.
N-CMW50000-A1- -1-i-1

| 0 | 100 | 200 | 300 | 400 | 500 Miles |
| 0 | 200 | 400 | 600 | 800 Kilometers |

Land Elevation: Feet (Meters)

9,840 and over (3,000 and over)	3,280 - 6,560 (1,000 - 2,000)	656 - 1,640 (200 - 500)
6,560 - 9,840 (2,000 - 3,000)	1,640 - 3,280 (500 - 1,000)	0 - 656 feet (0 - 200)

Europe Facts

Area: 3,800,000 square miles (9,900,000 square kilometers)

Highest Mountain: gora El'brus, Russia, 18,510 feet (5,642 meters)

Lowest Point: Caspian Sea, Russia, -92 feet (-28 meters)

Longest River: Volga, Russia, 2,290 miles (3,685 kilometers)

Largest Lake: Caspian Sea, Europe-Asia, 143,240 square miles (370,990 square kilometers)

Largest Island: Great Britain, 88,795 square miles (229,978 square kilometers)

THE LAND

Europe has a mild climate, a wealth of natural resources, and numerous rivers that have contributed to smooth and profitable trade between countries for centuries. These factors have also made European countries some of the wealthiest in the world. Most are able to sustain mixed economies based on many types of trade and manufacture, rather than only one or two.

Soaring, jagged peaks provide a striking backdrop for hikers in the French Alps.

Economies

European countries have traded freely with each other since the 1950s, when the first common market was established. More recently, the countries of eastern Europe have also begun competing in the open marketplace. In 1999, the European Union introduced the Euro, a unit of money that can be used in all member countries.

Economies
- Little or no activity
- Nomadic herding
- Hunting, forestry, subsistence farming
- Forestry
- Agriculture
- Stock raising
- Manufacturing, commerce
- Fishing

Environments
- Forest
- Swamp
- Crop and woodland
- Cropland
- Crop and grazing land
- Grassland
- Desert
- Tundra
- Barren
- Urban

Environments

Europe's environments range from frozen tundra and jagged mountains to grasslands and balmy beaches. Heavy industry and large human populations have polluted many land areas and waterways, but clean-up efforts are underway.

Arctic Circle

Stockholm
Moscow
London
Paris
Madrid
Rome
Bucharest

© Rand McNally

Arctic Circle

Murmansk
Arkhangel'sk
Stockholm
Moscow
London
Paris
Volgograd
Belgrade
Bucharest
Madrid
Rome

© Rand McNally

Climate

Tropical
- Rain all year
- Seasonal rain

Dry
- Desert
- Some rain

Moderate
- Dry summer
- Humid summer
- Rainy summer

Continental
- Long summer
- Short summer
- Very short, cool summer

Polar
- Tundra
- Ice cap

Highlands
- Varies with elevation

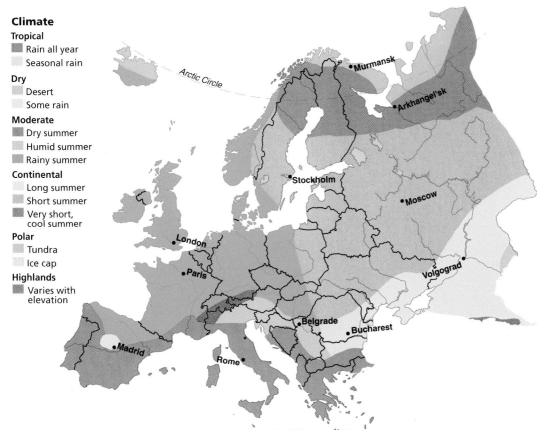

Arctic Circle · Murmansk · Arkhangel'sk · Stockholm · Moscow · London · Paris · Volgograd · Belgrade · Bucharest · Madrid · Rome

© Rand McNally

Climate

In western Europe, warm ocean air creates a climate far milder than northern lands elsewhere in the world. The currents don't affect eastern Europe, which experiences very cold winters. The Mediterranean climate of southern Europe has mild, wet winters and hot, dry summers.

In Denmark, a worker unloads a catch of sand eels from the North Sea.

Mining and Manufacturing

Europe's abundance of mineral resources, especially its coal, iron, and nickel reserves, fueled the Industrial Revolution of the 18th and 19th centuries and continues to supply the continent's industries today.

Germany is well-known for manufacturing automobiles with state-of-the art equipment.

Fishing and Farming

Western Europe's deeply etched coastline has long encouraged a healthy fishing industry. The European Plain supports some of the world's most fruitful farmland, while the climates and soils in Portugal, France, and Italy are perfect for growing grapes for fine wine.

Tourism

Thanks to their rich histories, pleasant climates, and stunning scenery, European countries are very popular tourist destinations. Today, many countries derive most of their income from tourist spending.

Tourists and natives enjoy the atmosphere of an outdoor cafe in Paris.

Forestry

Europe used to be covered with trees, but over the centuries many forests have been cleared for farms, cities, and manufacturing plants. There are still vast forests in Norway, Sweden, and Finland, which have large paper and wood-products industries.

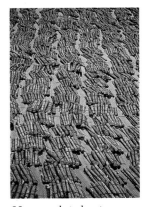

Harvested timber is transported on inland waterways to mills, where it is processed.

THE PEOPLE

Although farming is an important part of Europe's economy, most Europeans live and work in cities. Europe may be a small continent, but its more than 40 countries feature a tremendous diversity of cultures. Differences in language, customs, food, clothing, and religion give each European country a distinct identity. In places such as Italy and Spain, regions within the same country have very different cultures.

Bullfighter in Spain

For much of its history, Europe has been a hotbed of wars and border disputes. Two world wars wracked the continent in the first half of the 20th century and left it divided into two major parts: the western capitalist countries and the eastern Communist countries, which were loosely controlled by the Soviet Union. After the 1991 breakup of the Soviet Union, countries in eastern Europe began to reunite with the politically and economically stable west, a process that has spawned more wars and social and ethnic unrest in many places.

Hungarian dancers celebrate Constitution Day in Budapest.

Meals in Italy's restaurants are often served outdoors.

Guards at the Tower of London are known as "Beefeaters."

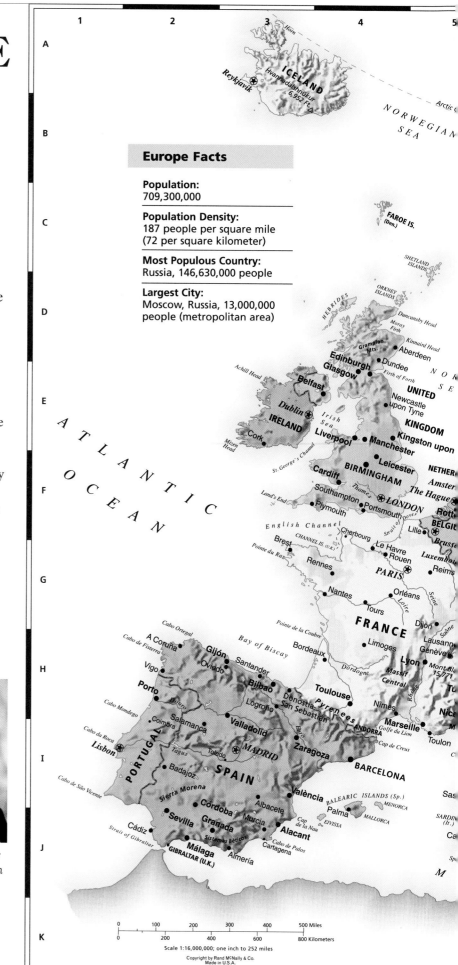

Europe Facts

Population:
709,300,000

Population Density:
187 people per square mile
(72 per square kilometer)

Most Populous Country:
Russia, 146,630,000 people

Largest City:
Moscow, Russia, 13,000,000 people (metropolitan area)

0   100   200   300   400   500 Miles
0   200   400   600   800 Kilometers
Scale 1:16,000,000; one inch to 252 miles

6　7　8　9　10　11　12　13

N
W · E
S

Nordkapp

BARENTS
SEA

Murmansk

Kol'skiy
poluostrov
Ponoy

Pechora

VESTERALEN

LOFOTEN

*Kebnekaise
6,926 Ft.*

Torneälven

White Sea

Arkhangel'sk

Ukhta

Mezen'

Ural Mountains

Severodvinsk

Oulu

FINLAND

Sevmaya Dvina

Syktykar

RUSSIA

Kotlas

*Kamskoye
vdkhr.*

PERM'

Trondheim

NORWAY

SWEDEN

*Gäsdhopiggen
8,100 Ft.*

Glåma

Oslo

Vaasa

Tampere

Petrozavodsk

Onezhskoye ozero

Sukhona

Kirov

Glazov

Votkinsk

Izhevsk

Naberezhnyye Chelny

Zlatoust

Gävle

Stockholm

Norrköping

Dalälven

Turku

Helsinki

Espoo

Gulf of Finland

ST. PETERSBURG

Cherepovets

*Rybinskoye
vdkhr.*

Vologda

Kostroma

*Gor'kovskoye
vdkhr.*

Rybinsk

Yaroslavl'

Ivanovo

**NIZHNIY
NOVGOROD**

KAZAN'

UFA

*Kuybyshevskoye
vdkhr.*

Kama

Uppsala

Vänern

Linköping

GOTLAND

Tallinn

ESTONIA

*Ladozhskoye
ozero*

Novgorod

*Chudskoye
ozero*

Tartu

Tver'

Dzerzhinsk

Cheboksary

Sterlitamak

Vättern

Göteborg

ÖLAND

Rīga

LATVIA

Pskov

Vladimir

Arzamas

Dimitrovgrad

MARK

Kattegat

Ålborg

Copenhagen

Malmö

Liepāja

Daugavpils

Velikiye Luki

MOSCOW

Noginsk
Kolomna
Oka

Ryazan'

Ul'yanovsk

Saransk

Tol'yatti

SAMARA

Orenburg

*BORNHOLM
(Den.)*

LITHUANIA

Klaipėda

Kaunas

Vitsyebsk

Smolensk

Serpukhov

Novomoskovsk

Kiel

Rostock

Gdańsk

RUSSIA

Kaliningrad

Vilnius

Neman

MINSK

Kaluga

Tula

Tambov

Saratov

Engel's

Balakovo

BREMER-
HAVEN

HAMBURG

Bremen

BERLIN

Szczecin

Wisla

Toruń

Białystok

Hrodna

Baranavichy

Mahilyow

Bryansk

Orel

Lipetsk

*Volgogradskoye
vdkhr.*

Hannover

GERMANY

Magdeburg

Poznań

POLAND

Oder

Brest

Homyel'

Chernihiv

Kursk

Belgorod

Voronezh

Kamyshin

Don

Essen

Leipzig

Łódź

WARSAW

Lublin

Pripyat

Mazyr

Pinsk

Sumy

KIEV

KHARKIV

Volzhskiy

*Tsimlyanskoye
vdkhr.*

Astrakhan'

Frankfurt

Dresden

Wrocław

Sudetes

Katowice

Rivne

Zhytomyr

UKRAINE

Poltava

Luhans'k

VOLGOGRAD

Volga

Mainz

PRAGUE

Plzeň

Ostrava

Kraków

L'viv

Vinnytsia

Kirovohrad

DNIPROPETROVS'K

Horlivka

Makiyivka

Novocherkassk

ROSTOV-NA-DONU

Elista

Nürnberg

Stuttgart

CZECH REPUBLIC

SLOVAKIA

Košice

Dniester

Ivano-Frankivs'k

Chernivtsi

Kryvyi Rih

Zaporizhzhia

DONETS'K

Mariupol'

Taganrog

sbourg

Zürich

*Lake
Constance*

MUNICH

Innsbruck

AUSTRIA

VIENNA

Bratislava

Győr

Miskolc

MOLDOVA

Iaşi

Mykolaïv

Kherson

Berdians'k

Sea of Azov

Krasnodar

Nevinnomyssk

Stavropol'

Pyatigorsk

Groznyy

Makhachkala

CASPIAN
SEA

ZERLAND

LIECH.

△*Grossglockner
12,461 Ft.*

Graz

HUNGARY

BUDAPEST

Debrecen

**Cluj-
Napoca**

Chişinău

Melitopol'

Kerch

Maykop

Nal'chik

Vladikavkaz

MILAN

Po

Ljubljana

SLOVENIA

Zagreb

Szeged

Drava

ROMANIA

Timişoara

ODESA

*Crimean
Peninsula*

Mys Tarkhankut

Novorossiysk

*gora El'brus
18,510 Ft.*

Caucasus

og

Bologna

Venice

CROATIA

BELGRADE

Carpathian Meridionali

Ploieşti

Simferopol'

Sevastopol'

La Spezia

SAN
MARINO

BOSNIA AND
HERZEGOVINA

YUGOSLAVIA

Craiova

BUCHAREST

Constanţa

BLACK SEA

Florence

Ancona

Split

Sarajevo

Niš

Danube

Ruse

Varna

ITALY

VATICAN CITY

Apennines

ADRIATIC SEA

Peć

SOFIA

BULGARIA

Plovdiv

Rhodope Mts.

ROME

ALBANIA

Skopje

MACEDONIA

Bari

*Vesuvius
4,190 Ft.*

Tiranë

Thessaloniki

*Ólimbos
9,570 Ft.*

Palermo

Messina

Taranto

Lecce

Pindhos Óros

NAPLES

Catanzaro

Cosenza

Capo Palinuro

*TYRRHENIAN
SEA*

Capo Colonna

GREECE

AEGEAN SEA

Catania

*Mt. Etna
10,902 Ft.*

*SICILY
(It.)*

*IONIAN
SEA*

Pátrai

Athens

RÓDHOS

*I. DI PANTELLERIA
(It.)*

Valletta

MALTA

CRETE

Iráklion

MEDITERRANEAN SEA

*A Greek fisherman
mends a handmade net.*

NORTHERN EUROPE

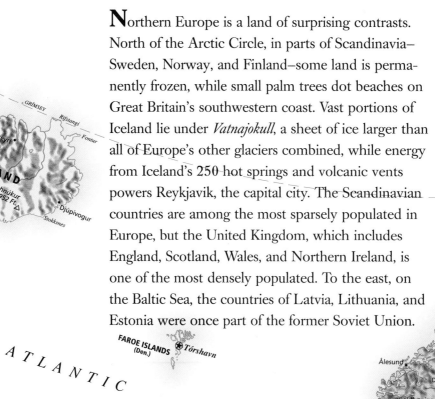

Northern Europe is a land of surprising contrasts. North of the Arctic Circle, in parts of Scandinavia– Sweden, Norway, and Finland–some land is perma- nently frozen, while small palm trees dot beaches on Great Britain's southwestern coast. Vast portions of Iceland lie under *Vatnajokull*, a sheet of ice larger than all of Europe's other glaciers combined, while energy from Iceland's 250 hot springs and volcanic vents powers Reykjavik, the capital city. The Scandinavian countries are among the most sparsely populated in Europe, but the United Kingdom, which includes England, Scotland, Wales, and Northern Ireland, is one of the most densely populated. To the east, on the Baltic Sea, the countries of Latvia, Lithuania, and Estonia were once part of the former Soviet Union.

Under the watchful eye of a shepherd, sheep graze on the green hills of Ireland.

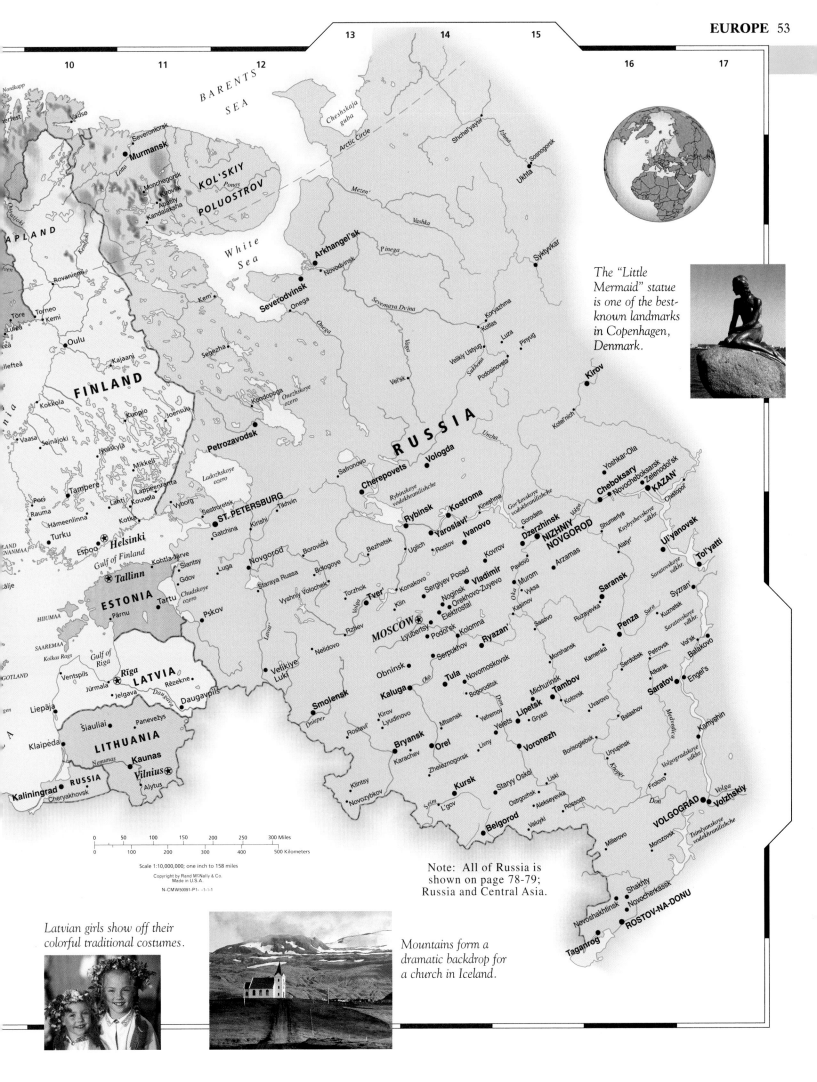

The "Little Mermaid" statue is one of the best-known landmarks in Copenhagen, Denmark.

Note: All of Russia is shown on page 78-79; Russia and Central Asia.

Latvian girls show off their colorful traditional costumes.

Mountains form a dramatic backdrop for a church in Iceland.

Scale 1:10,000,000; one inch to 158 miles

Copyright by Rand McNally & Co.
Made in U.S.A.
N-CMW50091-P1- -1-1-1

WESTERN AND CENTRAL EUROPE

Portuguese fisherman work on their nets before heading out to sea.

The cultures of western and central Europe are numerous and diverse, from the Islamic flavor of Spain's ancient Moorish cities to the sophisticated atmosphere of chic boutiques and sidewalk cafes in Paris, France. The region includes both the stunning beauty of the Swiss Alps and the heavy industry of Germany's Ruhr Valley. The slow, simple pace of life in a picturesque Italian hill town stands in contrast to the frenzied activity in the financial and political centers of Belgium and the Netherlands. Some of the smallest countries in the world are in this region: Andorra, San Marino, Monaco, and Vatican City, which is a tiny country entirely surrounded by the city of Rome, Italy.

Schönbrunn Palace in Vienna, Austria, was built for the Hapsburgs, a family that once ruled Austria, Germany, Spain, and other parts of Europe.

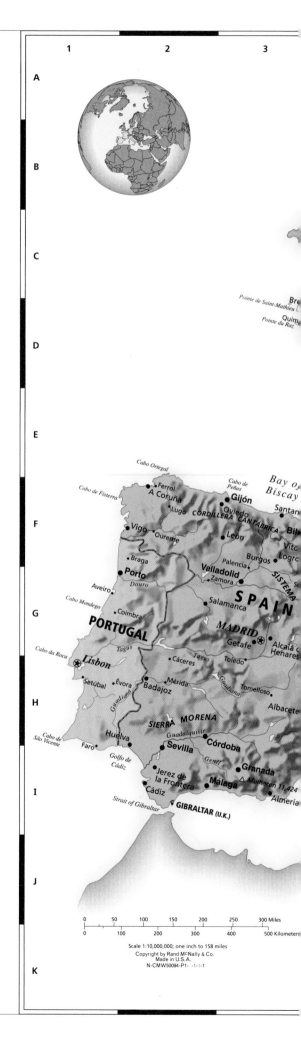

Scale 1:10,000,000; one inch to 158 miles
Copyright by Rand McNally & Co.
Made in U.S.A.
N-CMW50094-P1- -1-1-1

4   5   6   7   8   9   10   11

NORTH SEA

Flensburg
Kiel
Kap Arkona
Bremerhaven
Lübeck
Rostock
Schwerin
Oldenburg
HAMBURG
Schwedt
Groningen
Bremen
NETHERLANDS
Hannover
BERLIN
Haarlem
Amsterdam
Braunschweig
Potsdam
Osnabrück
Elbe
The Hague
Arnhem
Münster
Bielefeld
Hildesheim
Magdeburg
Rotterdam
Dessau
Brugge
Tilburg
Essen
Dortmund
Göttingen
Halle
Cottbus
Gent
Antwerpen
Maastricht
Wuppertal
Kassel
Leipzig
Dresden
Lille
BELGIUM
Düsseldorf
Siegen
Erfurt
Chemnitz
Lens
Brussels
Liège
Köln
Bonn
GERMANY
Zwickau
ORE MTS.
Cherbourg
Dieppe
Namur
Charleroi
Koblenz
Rhine
LUX.
Mainz
Frankfurt
Golfe de Saint-Malo
Le Havre
Rouen
Oise
Luxembourg
Trier
Wiesbaden
Main
Würzburg
BOHEMIAN FOREST
Caen
Évreux
Seine
Reims
Metz
Saarbrücken
Heilbronn
Nürnberg
Saint-Malo
Chartres
PARIS
Châlons-sur-Marne
Nancy
Karlsruhe
Regensburg
Danube
Rennes
Laval
Marne
Chaumont
Strasbourg
Stuttgart
Linz
Le Mans
Orléans
Troyes
BLACK FOREST
Augsburg
MUNICH
VIENNA
Angers
Tours
Loire
Vierzon
Nevers
Dijon
Mulhouse
Freiburg
Bodensee
Salzburg
Inn
AUSTRIA
Saint-Nazaire
Nantes
FRANCE
Poitiers
Besançon
Basel
Zürich
LIECHTENSTEIN
Innsbruck
Graz
La Rochelle
Saône
JURA
Luzern
SWITZERLAND
△ *Grossglockner 12,461 Ft.*
Klagenfurt
Limoges
Clermont-Ferrand
Villeurbanne
Geneva
Lausanne
Dufourspitze 15,203 Ft.
Bern
ALPS
Merano
Bolzano
Périgueux
Dordogne
Saint Étienne
Lyon
Mt. Blanc 15,771 Ft. △
△ *Matterhorn 14,692 Ft.*
Como
Trento
Udine
Cap Ferret
Bordeaux
Garonne
Aurillac
MASSIF
Grenoble
Novara
Bergamo
Brescia
Trieste
Lot
Montauban
CENTRAL
Valence
Rhône
Novara
MILAN
Verona
Venice
Mont-de-Marsan
PYRENEES
Pau
Montpellier
Nîmes
Turin
Piacenza
Parma
Ferrara
Tanaro
Donostia-San Sebastián
Toulouse
Monte Viso 12,602 Ft. △
Genoa
Bologna
Po
Pamplona
Perpignan
Aix-en-Provence
Savona
ANDORRA
Huesca
Nice
Golfo di Genova
Ravenna
Rimini
Zaragoza
Sabadell
Girona
Marseille
MONACO
La Spezia
Pisa
Florence
SAN MARINO
Toulon
Cannes
LIGURIAN SEA
Livorno
Ancona
Ebro
BARCELONA
Golfe du Lion
Cap Corse
Cap de Creus
Piombino
Siena
Perugia
ADRIATIC SEA
Bastia
CORSICA (Fr.)
ISOLA D'ELBA
ITALY
Terni
Pescara
Castelló de la Plana
BALEARIC ISLANDS (Sp.)
MENORCA
Ajaccio
Monte Rotondo 8,602 Ft. △
VATICAN CITY
ROME
APENNINES
ncia
Olbia
Str. of Bonifacio
San Severo
Foggia
Barletta
Cap de la Nau
Palma
MALLORCA
EIVISSA
Capo Caccia
Sassari
Capo Comino
Terracina
NAPLES
Ofanto
Bari
Brindisi
cant
Cap de Ses Salines
SARDINIA (It.)
Vesuvius 4,190 Ft. △
Salerno
Taranto
Lecce
cia
Cap de FORMENTERA
Punta La Marmora 6,017 Ft. △
TYRRHENIAN SEA
Capo Palinuro
Golfo di Taranto
Strait of Otranto
Cabo de Palos
gena
Iglesias
Cagliari
Capo Carbonara
Cosenza
Crotone
Capo Colonna
Capo Spartivento
Capo Vaticano
Catanzaro
IONIAN SEA
MEDITERRANEAN SEA
Trapani
Messina
Reggio di Calabria
Palermo
SICILY
Mt. Etna 10,902 Ft. △
Catania
Agrigento
Siracusa
Capo Passero
ISOLA DI PANTELLERIA (It.)
MALTA
Valletta

An Italian farmer inspects his grape crop.

The Colosseum in Rome was built nearly 2,000 years ago.

During the annual Grand Prix, racecars speed through the streets of Monte Carlo in Monaco.

N
W   E
S

Ibexes, a type of wild goat, graze on a hillside in Switzerland.

EASTERN EUROPE

In recent years, great changes have swept across Eastern Europe. From 1989 to 1991, the country known as the Soviet Union broke apart, and all 15 of its former republics–including Belarus, Ukraine, and Moldova–became independent countries. Then, in 1993, the country called Czechoslovakia split into two separate countries: the Czech Republic and Slovakia. These newly independent republics have worked to prosper in free market trade. Industry is thriving in Poland and Hungary, while others republics like Moldova and Slovakia remain largely agricultural.

Prague, in the Czech Republic, is one of Europe's loveliest and most historic cities.

The farmlands of Ukraine produce such bountiful harvests that this region is often referred to as the "Breadbasket of Europe."

Although the Carpathian Mountains skirt the borders of Poland, Slovakia, and Ukraine, most of Eastern Europe lies on the Great Northern European Plain where there is an abundance of fertile land. The beauty and mild weather of the Crimean Peninsula, which juts into the Black Sea, makes Ukraine a popular beach destination for tourists.

Kiev, the capital of Ukraine, straddles both sides of the Dnieper River.

The Tatra Mountains are the primary range of the Carpathian Mountains.

Hungary's Magyar people have been breeding horses for centuries.

Since World War II, Poland has had few minority groups. Today, its people have a very strong national identity.

BALTIC SEA

Polatsk

Vitsyebsk

Gdynia
Gdańsk
Koszalin
Tczew
Elbląg
Suwałki
Maladzyechna
Barysaw
Orsha
MINSK
Mahilyow

Szczecin
Olsztyn
Lida
Hrodna
BELARUS
Krychaw

Grudziądz
Neman

Gorzów
Wielkopolski
Bydgoszcz
Toruń
Łomża
Białystok
Baranavichy
Babruysk

Zielona Góra
Włocławek
Slonim
Slutsk
Homyel'

Poznań
Warta
Wisła
WARSAW
Pinsk
Pripyat
Mazyr
Hlukhiv

Głogów
Kalisz
Łódź
POLAND
Siedlce
Brest
Kobryn
Chernihiv

Legnica
Piotrków
Trybunalski
Radom
Lublin
Kovel'
Syr
Korosten'
Chornobyl'
Konotop
Sumy

Wrocław
Wałbrzych
Częstochowa
Chełm
Luts'k
Rivne
Nizhyn
Pryluky

Liberec
SUDETES
Opole
Zabr Buh
Dubno
KIEV
Okhtyrka
KHARKIV

Cheb
Kladno
PRAGUE
Bytom
Sosnowiec
Kielce
Rzeszów
San
L'viv
Zhytomyr
Berdychiv
Bila Tserkva
Lubny
Poltava
Izium
Kupians'k
Sieverodonets'k

Plzeň
CZECH REPUBLIC
Sumperk
Ostrava
Kraków
Bielsko-Biała
Krosno
Ternopil'
Khmel'nyts'kyi
Cherkasy
Kremenchuk
Slovians'k
Kramators'k
Luhans'k

Pisek
Olomouc
Žilina
Sambir
Ivano-Frankivs'k
Vinnytsia
Kremenchuts'ke vdskh.
UKRAINE
Stakhanov
Alchevs'k
Krasnyi Luch

České
Budějovice
Brno
Trenčín
Poprad
Prešov
CARPATHIAN MOUNTAINS
Uman'
Oleksandriia
Dniprodzerzhyns'k
Horlivka
Makiivka

Prievidza
Kirovohrad
DNIPROPETROVS'K
DONETS'K
Novoshakhtinsk

BOHEMIAN FOREST
SLOVAKIA
Banská
Bystrica
Košice
Uzhhorod
Mohyliv-
Podil's'kyi
Kryvyi Rih
Kotovs'k
Pivdenyy Buh
Voznesens'k
Zaporizhzhia
Nikopol'
Mariupol'

Bratislava
Trnava
Győr
Gyöngyös
Miskolc
Berehove
Chernivtsi
MOLDOVA
Orhei
Mykolaïv
Dnipro
Melitopol'
Berdians'k

Székesfehérvár
BUDAPEST
Debrecen
Nyíregyháza
Chişinău
Tighina
Tiraspol
ODESA
Kherson
SEA OF AZOV

HUNGARY
Kecskemét
Prut
Dnister
Bălţi

Kaposvár
Tisza
Szeged
Bilhorod-
Dnistrovs'kyi
Dzhankoi
Kerch

Pécs
Dráva
Danube
Cahul
Kiliya
Mys
Tarkhankut
Ievpatoriia
**CRIMEAN
PENINSULA**
Simferopol'

Sevastopol'
Mys Sarych
Yalta

BLACK SEA

0 50 100 150 200 250 300 Miles
0 100 200 300 400 500 Kilometers

Scale 1:10,000,000; one inch to 158 miles
Copyright by Rand McNally & Co.
Made in U.S.A.
N-CMW50093-P1- -1- -1-

SOUTHEASTERN EUROPE

Except for Greece, Southeastern Europe was controlled by the Soviet Union for much of the 20th century. Since the Soviet Union broke apart in 1989-1991, the countries of Southeastern Europe have embraced their newfound freedom. However, some of them have also struggled to accommodate the many ethnic and religious differences that exist among their inhabitants. In Bosnia and Herzegovina, as well as in Yugoslavia, these tensions erupted into outright war. Today the region remains unstable, despite the diplomatic efforts of the United Nations and the international community.

Albanian refugees flee the fighting in Kosovo.

This castle in the Transylvania region of northwestern Romania inspired Dracula, *the famous story about a blood-sucking count.*

Some 2,500 years ago, the city-states of ancient Greece represented one of the most highly developed and influential civilizations the world has ever known. Today, Greece takes advantage of its lengthy sea coast to launch one of the world's largest merchant fleets, while its mild climate, impressive history, and lovely scenery make tourism an important part of the national economy.

The Karawanken Mountains rise behind an 11th century castle in Slovenia.

Whitewashed homes overlook the sea on the Greek island of Santorini.

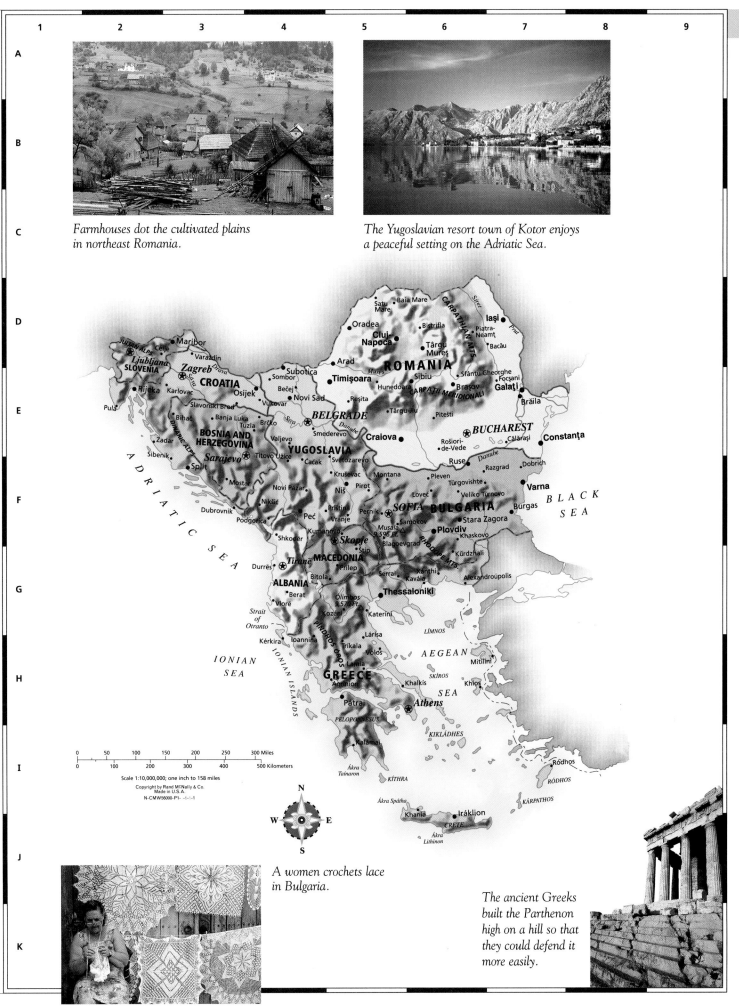

Farmhouses dot the cultivated plains
in northeast Romania.

The Yugoslavian resort town of Kotor enjoys
a peaceful setting on the Adriatic Sea.

SLOVENIA

Maribor
Celje
Ljubljana
Varaždin
Zagreb
CROATIA
Rijeka
Karlovac
Pula
Osijek
Slavonski Brod
Bihać
Banja Luka
Tuzla
Brčko
Zadar
BOSNIA AND
HERZEGOVINA
Šibenik
Sarajevo
Split
Valjevo
Mostar

Satu
Mare
Baia Mare
Oradea
Bistrița
Cluj-
Napoca
Târgu
Mureș
Arad
ROMANIA
Subotica
Sombor
Timișoara
Sibiu
Bečej
Reșița
Hunedoara
Novi Sad
BELGRADE
CARPAȚII MERIDIONALI
Târgu-Jiu
Smederevo
Craiova
YUGOSLAVIA
Titovo Užice
Čačak
Svetozarevo
Ruse
Kruševac
Novi Pazar
Niš
Pirot
Montana
Nikšić
Dubrovnik
Podgorica
Peć
Prishtina
Vranje
Pernik
Kumanovo
Skopje
Štip
Shkodër
Tiranë
MACEDONIA
Prilep
Durrës
Bitola
ALBANIA
Berat
Vlorë

Iași
Piatra-
Neamț
Bacău
Sfântu Gheorghe
Focșani
Brașov
Galați
Pitești
Brăila
BUCHAREST
Rošiori-
de-Vede
Constanța
Danube
Razgrad
Dobrich
Pleven
Târgovishte
Varna
Lovec
Veliko Tŭrnovo
SOFIA BULGARIA
Burgas
Samokov
Stara Zagora
Musala
9,596 Ft.
Plovdiv
Khaskovo
Blagoevgrad
Kŭrdzhali
RHODOPE MTS.
Xanthi
Serrai
Kavála
Alexandroúpolis
Thessaloniki
Olimbos
9,570 Ft.
Kozáni
Katerini

CARPATHIAN MTS.
Prut
Sirel
Mureș
Drava
Sava
Danube
Sava

ADRIATIC SEA
DINARIC ALPS
JULIAN ALPS

BLACK
SEA

Strait
of
Otranto
Kérkira
Ioánnina
IONIAN
SEA
IONIAN ISLANDS
PINDHOS OROS
Trikala
Lárisa
Vólos
GREECE
Agrínion
Pátrai
Lamía
Khalkís
Athens
PELOPONNESUS
KIKLÁDHES
Kalámai
Ákra
Taínaron
KÍTHRA
LÍMNOS
Mitilíni
SKÍROS
AEGEAN
SEA
Khíos
Ákra Spátha
Khaniá
Iráklion
CRETE
Ákra
Líthinon
Ródhos
RÓDHOS
KÁRPATHOS

0 50 100 150 200 250 300 Miles
0 100 200 300 400 500 Kilometers
Scale 1:10,000,000; one inch to 158 miles
Copyright by Rand McNally & Co.
Made in U.S.A.
N-CMW56000-P1- -1-1-1

N
W   E
S

A women crochets lace
in Bulgaria.

The ancient Greeks
built the Parthenon
high on a hill so that
they could defend it
more easily.

AFRICA

Africa, the world's second-largest continent, is a land of dramatic and varied terrain. Narrow plains line the coast, while wide plateaus fill much of the continent's interior. Lush tropical rain forests flank the equator near the center of the continent. Sun-scorched deserts span the north and portions of the southwest, and grasslands called savannas lie between the deserts and the rain forests.

Across this vast continent are great rivers, mountains, and valleys. It contains four major rivers, but the Nile–the longest in the world–is the most important. It flows north across more than half of the continent before emptying into the Mediterranean Sea. Africa's mountain ranges include some majestic peaks such as Kilimanjaro in Tanzania. Between the mountain ranges of eastern Africa lies the Rift Valley, a long rip in the earth's surface that extends about 4,000 miles (almost 6,500 kilometers) and contains volcanoes, hot springs, and some of the world's largest and deepest lakes.

Egypt's ancient pyramids (above) have withstood the test of time; the African lion (left) is often called "King of Beasts"; Kilimanjaro (below) rises above the Amboseli Plain in Kenya.

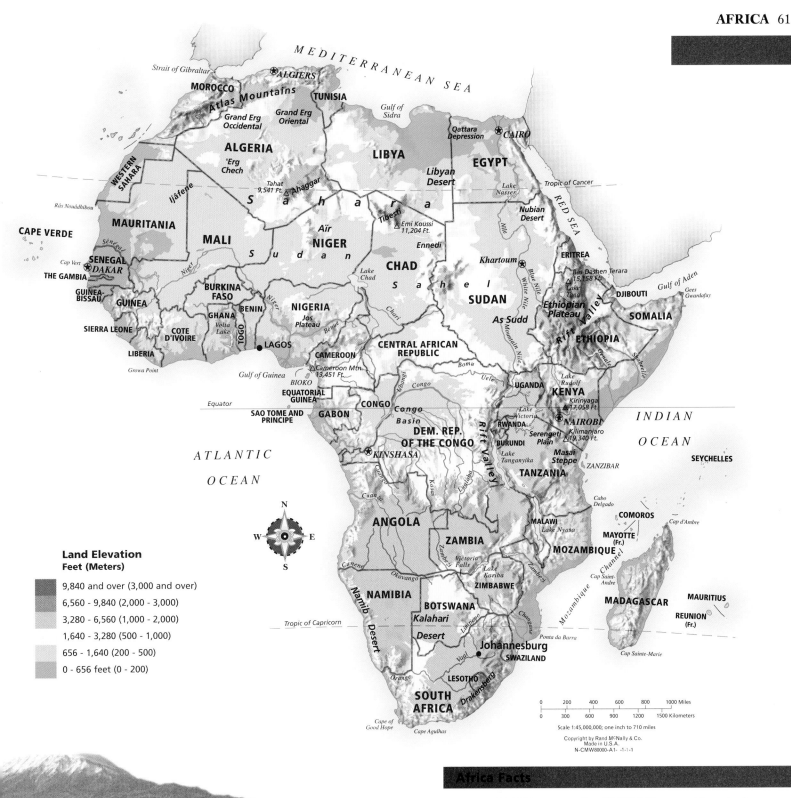

MEDITERRANEAN SEA

Strait of Gibraltar

MOROCCO
Atlas Mountains
TUNISIA
ALGERIERS
Grand Erg
Occidental
Grand Erg
Oriental
Gulf of
Sidra
Qattara
Depression
CAIRO

ALGERIA
LIBYA
EGYPT
Libyan
Desert

'Erg
Chech
Tahat
9,541 Ft.
Ahaggar
Tropic of Cancer
Lake
Nasser

WESTERN
SAHARA
Ijâfene
S a h a r a
Nubian
Desert

Râs Nouâdhibou

CAPE VERDE
MAURITANIA
MALI
Aïr
NIGER
Tibesti
Emi Koussi
11,204 Ft.
Ennedi
CHAD
Khartoum
RED SEA
Ras Dashen Terara
15,158 Ft.
ERITREA
Lake
Tana
Gulf of Aden
Gees
Gwardafuy

Cap Vert
SENEGAL
DAKAR
Senegal
S u d a n
Lake
Chad
S a h e l
Nile
Blue Nile
White Nile
DJIBOUTI
SOMALIA

THE GAMBIA
Niger
BURKINA
FASO
Niger
NIGERIA
SUDAN
As Sudd
Chari
Ethiopian
Plateau
ETHIOPIA

GUINEA-
BISSAU
GUINEA
BENIN
Jos
Plateau
Benue
Rift Valley

SIERRA LEONE
GHANA
Volta
Lake
TOGO

COTE
D'IVOIRE
LAGOS
CAMEROON
CENTRAL AFRICAN
REPUBLIC
Bomu
Uele
UGANDA
Lake
Rudolf
KENYA
Kirinyaga
17,058 Ft.

LIBERIA
Growa Point
BIOKO
Cameroon Mtn.
13,451 Ft.
Ubangi
Congo
Lake
Victoria
NAIROBI
Kilimanjaro
19,340 Ft.
Shebelle
Genale

Gulf of Guinea
EQUATORIAL
GUINEA
CONGO
Congo
Basin
RWANDA
Serengeti
Plain
INDIAN
OCEAN

Equator
SAO TOME AND
PRINCIPE
GABON
DEM. REP.
OF THE CONGO
BURUNDI
Masai
Steppe
ZANZIBAR

ATLANTIC

OCEAN
KINSHASA
Lukenie
Kasai
Lake
Tanganyika
TANZANIA
SEYCHELLES

Cuanza
Lualaba
Cabo
Delgado

ANGOLA
COMOROS
Cap d'Ambre

N
W E
S
ZAMBIA
MALAWI
Lake Nyasa
MAYOTTE
(Fr.)

Land Elevation
Feet (Meters)
Cunene
Okavango
Zambezi
Victoria
Falls
Lake
Kariba
MOZAMBIQUE
Zambezi
Mozambique Channel
Cap Saint-
Andre
MADAGASCAR
MAURITIUS

9,840 and over (3,000 and over)
ZIMBABWE
REUNION
(Fr.)

6,560 - 9,840 (2,000 - 3,000)
Namib Desert
NAMIBIA
BOTSWANA
Kalahari
Desert
Limpopo
Chobe
Ponta da Barra

3,280 - 6,560 (1,000 - 2,000)
Tropic of Capricorn
Cap Sainte-Marie

1,640 - 3,280 (500 - 1,000)
Johannesburg
SWAZILAND

656 - 1,640 (200 - 500)
Orange
Vaal
LESOTHO
Drakensberg

0 - 656 feet (0 - 200)
SOUTH
AFRICA
Cape of
Good Hope
Cape Agulhas

0 200 400 600 800 1000 Miles
0 300 600 900 1200 1500 Kilometers
Scale 1:45,000,000; one inch to 710 miles
Copyright by Rand McNally & Co.
Made in U.S.A.
N-CMW80000-A1- -1-1-1

Africa Facts

Area: 11,700,000 square miles (30,300,000 square kilometers)

Highest Mountain: Kilimanjaro, Tanzania, 19,340 feet (5,895 meters)

Lowest Point: Lac Assal, Djibouti, -515 feet (-157 meters)

Longest River: Nile, 4,145 miles (6,671 kilometers) —world's longest river

Largest Lake: Lake Victoria, Kenya-Tanzania-Uganda, 26,820 square miles (69,463 square kilometers)

Largest Desert: Sahara, northern Africa, 3,500,000 square miles (9,065,000 square kilometers)—world's largest desert

Largest Island: Madagascar, 226,500 square miles (587,000 square kilometers)

THE LAND

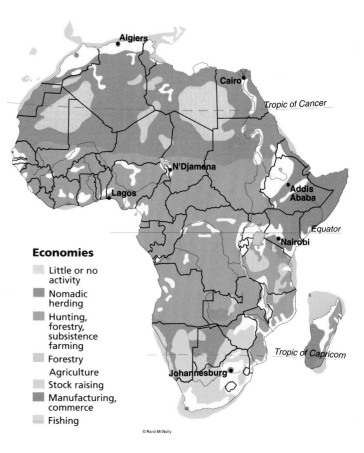

The land in Africa offers up an assortment of riches–from gold and minerals found deep within the earth to the crops that grow at its surface. Different industries dominate different parts of the continent: Economic activity depends on the quality of the land and variations in regional climate. Many African countries depend on a single industry to drive the economy, but people in other areas are looking for new ways to make the most of their natural resources.

Economies

Economies
- Little or no activity
- Nomadic herding
- Hunting, forestry, subsistence farming
- Forestry
- Agriculture
- Stock raising
- Manufacturing, commerce
- Fishing

Economies

Most Africans are either farmers or herders. Many live as their ancestors did for thousands of years, continually moving across the land to follow animal herds, or living in small villages, raising crops and animals.

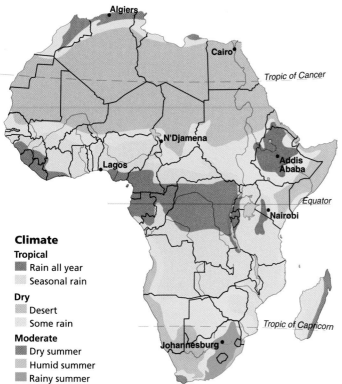

Climate
Tropical
- Rain all year
- Seasonal rain

Dry
- Desert
- Some rain

Moderate
- Dry summer
- Humid summer
- Rainy summer

Continental
- Long summer
- Short summer
- Very short, cool summer

Polar
- Tundra
- Ice cap

Highlands
- Varies with elevation

Climates

Africa is the world's hottest continent. One-third of Africa's land area is desert, but near the equator a tremendous amount of rain falls. The tropical rain forests of central Africa are hot and humid.

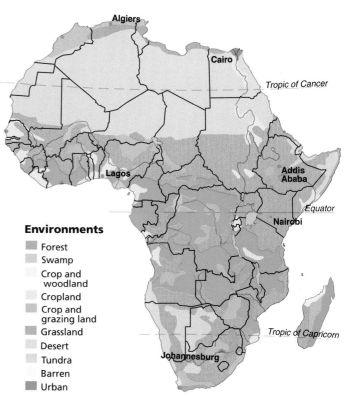

Environments
- Forest
- Swamp
- Crop and woodland
- Cropland
- Crop and grazing land
- Grassland
- Desert
- Tundra
- Barren
- Urban

Mining

Africa has some of the largest mineral reserves in the world, most of them untapped. The world's largest uranium mine is in Namibia, and copper is Zambia's major export. There are extensive oil fields in the forbidding deserts of northern Africa, and large gold, platinum, and diamond mines in South Africa.

World Gold Production

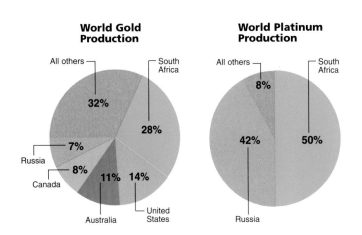

All others — 32%
South Africa — 28%
Russia — 7%
Canada — 8%
Australia — 11%
United States — 14%

World Platinum Production

All others — 8%
South Africa — 50%
Russia — 42%

This open-air bazaar in Algeria is a thriving marketplace.

Farming

Three out of four Africans work in agriculture. There are two major types of farming in Africa. The first is subsistence farming, when people grow enough food to feed themselves and their families. The second is commercial farming, when major companies grow large quantities of crops for sale. Commercial farms throughout central and southern Africa produce crops such as coffee, bananas, tobacco, and cocoa. Some of these items are sold only in African markets. Other yields, called cash crops, are grown specifically for canning, freezing, or refining, and are sold overseas.

Africa possesses approximately 40 percent of the world's hydroelectric potential. Kenya's Lake Kariba Dam provides power for the surrounding region.

Johannesburg is a prosperous South African city.

Tourism

Tourism is a major industry for many African countries that are not industrialized. Every year, hundreds of thousands of people flock to the deserts of Egypt to see the colossal pyramids and the mighty Sphinx, built thousands of years ago. The wildlife preserves in Kenya and Tanzania attract thousands of people from around the world who come to see and photograph the magnificent wildlife that lives there.

The Great Sphinx of Egypt is one of Africa's most-hallowed tourist destinations.

THE PEOPLE

Africa's more than 50 countries represent a complex mixture of peoples and cultures, with hundreds of ethnic groups and at least 1,000 different languages. For thousands of years, Africans organized themselves into tribal nations. From the 1600s into the 1960s, Europeans colonized most of the continent, but today the colonies are gone and nearly every country is independent. Although civil war has torn apart many of these countries, and Africa's population continues to face great challenges, the continent remains a place of opportunity due to the diversity of its cultures and resourcefulness of its people.

Schoolchildren wave the flag of South Africa on the steps of Parliament.

Masai women from Kenya wear colorful, traditional native dress.

A young woman walks among a herd of camels in Morocco.

In Burundi, men form a ceremonial circle to play tambor drums.

Africans travel and transport goods by camel because the animals are well adapted to desert life.

A little girl stands in front of a restaurant in a small town in Namibia.

The Arabian sitar is a popular musical instrument in northern Africa.

MEDITERRANEAN SEA

Strait of Gibraltar
ALGIERS
Rabat
CASABLANCA
Wahran
Qacentina
Tunis
MOROCCO
TUNISIA
Marrakech
Ghardaïa
Tripoli
Gulf of Sidra
Banghāzī
ALEXANDRIA
CAIRO
Suez

ALGERIA
LIBYA
EGYPT
Asyūt

El Aaiún
Aswān
Lake Nasser

WESTERN SAHARA
Tropic of Cancer

CAPE VERDE
MAURITANIA
Nouakchott
MALI
NIGER
CHAD
Port Sudan
RED SEA

Senegal
Timbuktu
Omdurman
Khartoum
ERITREA
Asmera
Gulf of Aden

DAKAR
SENEGAL
Niger
Niamey
Kano
N'Djamena
Lake Chad
SUDAN
Lake Tana
DJIBOUTI
Djibouti

THE GAMBIA
Bamako
BURKINA FASO
Ouagadougou
NIGERIA
Chari
Blue Nile
ADDIS ABABA
SOMALIA

GUINEA-BISSAU
GUINEA
BENIN
Abuja
Benue
CENTRAL AFRICAN REPUBLIC
Bangui
Bomu
Mountain Nile
ETHIOPIA

Conakry
Freetown
COTE D'IVOIRE
GHANA
TOGO
Cotonou
LAGOS
CAMEROON
Bangui
Omo

SIERRA LEONE
Monrovia
Volta Lake
Accra
DOUALA
Uele
UGANDA
Lake Rudolf
Mogadishu

LIBERIA
ABIDJAN
EQUATORIAL GUINEA
Yaoundé
Congo
Kisangani
Kampala
KENYA
Equator

SAO TOME AND PRINCIPE
Libreville
CONGO
DEM. REP. OF THE CONGO
RWANDA
Kigali
Lake Victoria
NAIROBI
INDIAN

GABON
Ubangi
Brazzaville
KINSHASA
Bujumbura
BURUNDI
Lubumbashi
TANZANIA
Mombasa
OCEAN

ATLANTIC
Congo
Lualaba
Dodoma
DAR ES SALAAM
SEYCHELLES

OCEAN
LUANDA
Cuango
Mbuji-Mayi
Lake Tanganyika

Lobito
ANGOLA
Lubumbashi
MALAWI
Lake Nyasa
COMOROS

Huambo
ZAMBIA
Ndola
Llongwe
MAYOTTE (Fr.)

Cunene
Lusaka
Lake Kariba
Zambezi
MOZAMBIQUE
ANTANANARIVO
MAURITIUS

NAMIBIA
Okavango
Harare
ZIMBABWE
Beira
MADAGASCAR
REUNION (Fr.)

Windhoek
BOTSWANA
Limpopo
Mozambique Channel
Tropic of Capricorn

Gaborone
Pretoria
MAPUTO
SWAZILAND

Orange
Johannesburg
LESOTHO
Maseru
Durban

SOUTH AFRICA

Cape Town
Port Elizabeth

N
W E
S

Africa Facts

Population:
770,300,000

Population Density:
66 people per square mile
(25 per square kilometer)

Most Populous Country:
Nigeria, 112,170,000 people

Largest City:
Cairo, Egypt, 13,250,000 people
(metropolitan area)

0   200   400   600   800   1000 Miles
0   300   600   900   1200   1500 Kilometers
Scale 1:45,000,000; one inch to 710 miles

Copyright by Rand McNally & Co.
Made in U.S.A.
N-CMW80000-P1- -1- -1

NORTHERN AFRICA

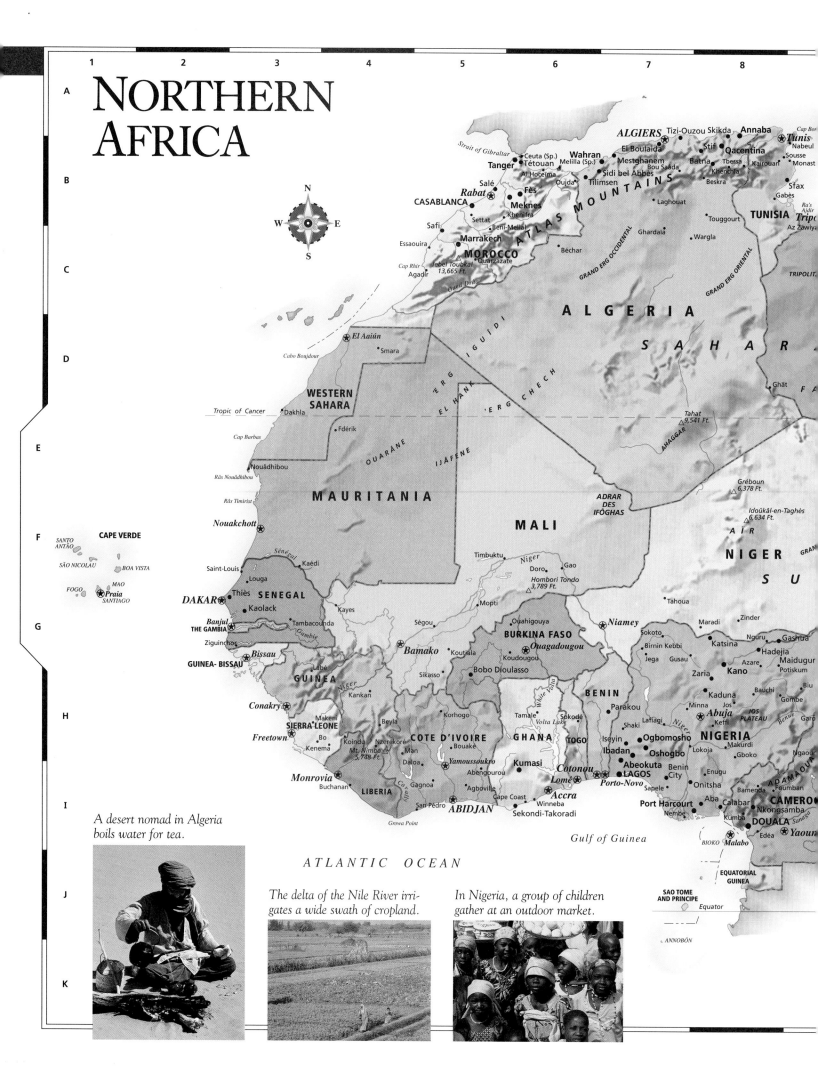

Strait of Gibraltar

ALGIERS   Tizi-Ouzou   Skikda   Annaba   Tunis
Ceuta (Sp.)   El Boulaida   Stif   Qacentina   Nabeul
Tanger   Tétouan   Melilla (Sp.)   Mestghanem   Batna   Tbessa   Sousse
Al Hoceïma   Wahran   Bou Saâda   Khenchla   Kairouan   Monast
Salé   Oujda   Sidi bel Abbès   Beskra
Rabat   Fès   Tilimsen   Sfax
CASABLANCA   Meknes   ATLAS MOUNTAINS   Laghouat   TUNISIA   Gabès
Khenifra   Touggourt   Ra's Ajdir
Safi   Settat   Beni-Mellal   Ghardaïa   Tripolit
Marrakech   Wargla   Az Zâwiya
Essaouira   Béchar   GRAND ERG OCCIDENTAL
MOROCCO
Cap Rhir   Jebel Toubkal 13,665 Ft.   Ouarzazate   GRAND ERG ORIENTAL   TRIPOLIT.
Agadir   ALGERIA
Oued Drâa   SAHARA

El Aaiún   Smara   ERG IGUIDI
Cabo Boujdour   ERG CHECH   Ghât
WESTERN SAHARA   EL HANK   FA
Tropic of Cancer   Dakhla
Cap Barbas   Fdérik   'ERG CHECH   Tahat △ 9,541 Ft.   AHAGGAR
OUARÂNE   IJÂFENE
Nouâdhibou   Gréboun △ 6,378 Ft.
Râs Nouâdhibou   ADRAR DES IFÔGHAS   Idoûkâl-en-Taghès 6,634 Ft.
Râs Timirist   MAURITANIA   AÏR
Nouakchott   MALI   NIGER
CAPE VERDE   SU   GRAN
SANTO ANTÃO
SÃO NICOLAU   BOA VISTA   Sénégal   Saint-Louis   Kaédi   Timbuktu   Niger   Doro   Gao
FOGO   MAIO   Louga   Hombori Tondo 3,789 Ft. △   Tahoua   Maradi   Zinder
Praia SANTIAGO   DAKAR   Thiès   SENEGAL   Kayes   Mopti   Sokoto   Nguru   Gashua
Kaolack   Ségou   Ouahigouya   Niamey   Birnin Kebbi   Katsina   Hadejia   Maidugur
Banjul   Tambacounda   BURKINA FASO   Jega   Gusau   Potiskum
THE GAMBIA   Gambie   Bamako   Koutiala   Ouagadougou   Zaria   Kano
Ziguinchor   Bobo Dioulasso   Kaduna   Bauchi   Biu
Bissau   Labé   Niger   Sikasso   BENIN   Minna   Jos   Gombe
GUINEA-BISSAU   Kankan   Parakou   Abuja   JOS PLATEAU
GUINEA   Korhogo   Tamale   Sokodé   Keffi   NIGERIA   Garo
Conakry   Beyla   Volta Lake   Shaki   Lafiagi   Benue
Makeni   White Volta   Iseyin   Ogbomosho   Makurdi   Ngaou
SIERRA LEONE   Bo   Koindu   Nzerekoré   COTE D'IVOIRE   GHANA   TOGO   Ibadan   Oshogbo   Lokoja   Gboko
Freetown   Kenema   Man   Bouaké   Yamoussoukro   Kumasi   Cotonou   Abeokuta   Benin City   Onitsha   Bamenda   Foumban
Mt. Nimba 5,748 Ft. △   Daloa   Lomé   LAGOS   Enugu   CAMER
Monrovia   Abengourou   Porto-Novo   Sapele   Aba   Calabar   Nkongsamba
Buchanan   Gagnoa   Accra   Port Harcourt   Kúmba   DOUALA
LIBERIA   Agboville   Cape Coast   Winneba   Nembe   Edéa   Yaoun
San Pédro   ABIDJAN   Sekondi-Takoradi   BIOKO   Malabo
Growa Point   Gulf of Guinea
EQUATORIAL GUINEA

A desert nomad in Algeria boils water for tea.

ATLANTIC OCEAN

The delta of the Nile River irrigates a wide swath of cropland.

In Nigeria, a group of children gather at an outdoor market.

SAO TOME AND PRINCIPE
Equator

ANNOBÓN

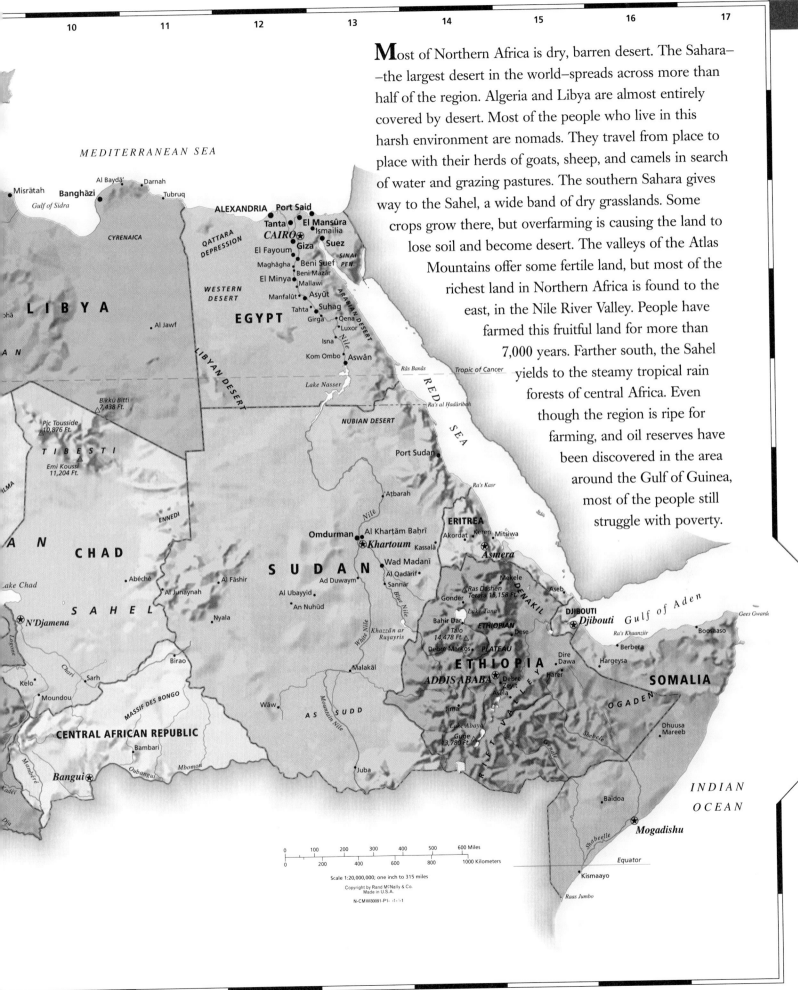

Most of Northern Africa is dry, barren desert. The Sahara—the largest desert in the world—spreads across more than half of the region. Algeria and Libya are almost entirely covered by desert. Most of the people who live in this harsh environment are nomads. They travel from place to place with their herds of goats, sheep, and camels in search of water and grazing pastures. The southern Sahara gives way to the Sahel, a wide band of dry grasslands. Some crops grow there, but overfarming is causing the land to lose soil and become desert. The valleys of the Atlas Mountains offer some fertile land, but most of the richest land in Northern Africa is found to the east, in the Nile River Valley. People have farmed this fruitful land for more than 7,000 years. Farther south, the Sahel yields to the steamy tropical rain forests of central Africa. Even though the region is ripe for farming, and oil reserves have been discovered in the area around the Gulf of Guinea, most of the people still struggle with poverty.

MEDITERRANEAN SEA

Misrātah Banghāzi Al Baydā' Darnah
Gulf of Sidra Tubruq
CYRENAICA
ALEXANDRIA Port Said
QATTARA DEPRESSION Tanta El Mansûra
CAIRO Ismailia
Giza Suez
El Fayoum Beni Suef SINAI PEN.
Maghâgha
El Minya Beni Mazâr
WESTERN DESERT Mallawi
Manfalût Asyût
Al Jawf Tahta Suhâg
Girga Qena
Luxor
LIBYA Isna
EGYPT
Kom Ombo
LIBYAN DESERT Aswân
Lake Nasser Râs Banâs Tropic of Cancer
Bikkü Bitti 7,438 Ft.
Pic Tousside 10,876 Ft. Ra's al Ḥadāribah
TIBESTI NUBIAN DESERT
Emi Koussi 11,204 Ft. RED SEA
Port Sudan
Ra's Kasr
ENNEDI 'Aṭbarah
CHAD ERITREA
Omdurman Al Khartām Bahrī Akordat Keren Mitsiwa
Khartoum Kassalā Asmera
SUDAN Wad Madani
Abéché Al Fāshir Ad Duwaym Al Qadārif Mekele
Lake Chad Al Junaynah Al Ubayyid Sannār Ras Dashen Aseb
N'Djamena An Nuhūd Gonder Terara 15,158 Ft. DENAKIL
SAHEL Nyala Bahir Dar Lake Tana DJIBOUTI Gulf of Aden
Birao ETHIOPIAN Djibouti Gees Gwardi
Kelo White Nile Blue Nile Tālo 14,478 Ft. Dese Ra's Khaanziir Boosaaso
Sarh Khazzân ar Ruşayris Debre Markos PLATEAU Berbeta
Moundou Dire Dawa Hargeysa
MASSIF DES BONGO ETHIOPIA
Malakāl ADDIS ABABA Debre Zeyit Harer SOMALIA
CENTRAL AFRICAN REPUBLIC Asela OGADEN
Bambari Wāw AS SUDD Jima Dhuusa Mareeb
Bangui Mbomou Lake Abaya Shebelle
Oubangui Guge 13,780 Ft.
Mountain Nile
INDIAN OCEAN
Juba
Baidoa
Shabeelle Mogadishu
Equator
Kismaayo
Raas Jumbo

0 100 200 300 400 500 600 Miles
0 200 400 600 800 1000 Kilometers
Scale 1:20,000,000; one inch to 315 miles
Copyright by Rand McNally & Co.
Made in U.S.A.
N-CMW80091-P1- -1- -1-1

SOUTHERN AFRICA

Cheetah

Like the land to the north, Southern Africa is known for a number of outstanding natural features. In the eastern part of the region, the Rift Valley, a great gash in the earth's surface, stretches about 4,000 miles (almost 6,500 kilometers) from Ethiopia south to Zambia. Mountain ranges rise along both sides of the Valley. In the surrounding savannas, or grasslands, large herds of zebras, elephants, rhinoceroses, giraffes, wildebeests, and other animals roam the land. South of the grasslands are the Kalahari and Namib Deserts. Most people in Southern Africa live in small villages, but the region also contains the major cities of Nairobi, Kenya, and Kinshasa, Democratic Republic of the Congo.

In Tanzania's Serengeti National Park, acacia trees rise up from the grasslands.

African animals come in all sizes and shapes:

Fennec Fox

Bongo

African Elephant

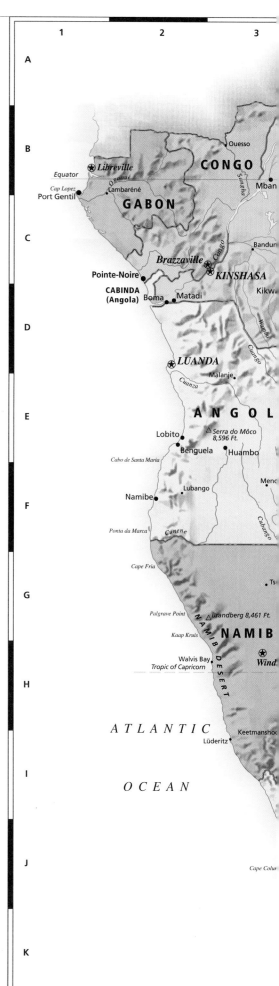

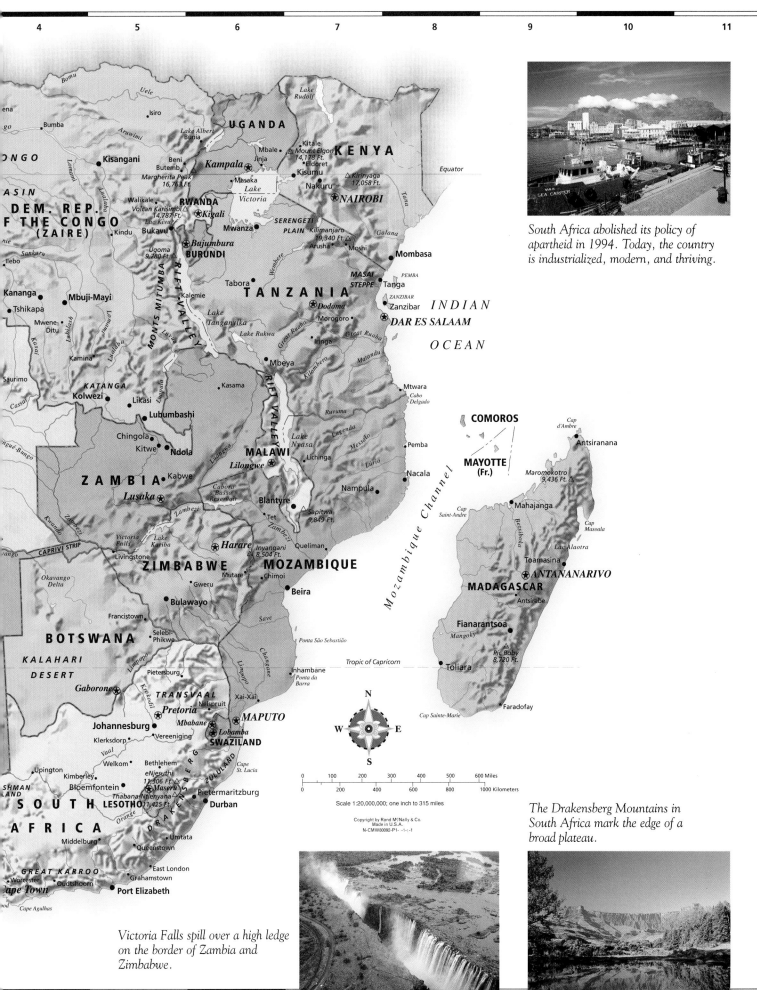

South Africa abolished its policy of apartheid in 1994. Today, the country is industrialized, modern, and thriving.

The Drakensberg Mountains in South Africa mark the edge of a broad plateau.

Victoria Falls spill over a high ledge on the border of Zambia and Zimbabwe.

Scale 1:20,000,000; one inch to 315 miles

Copyright by Rand McNally & Co.
Made in U.S.A.
N-CMW80092-P1- -1-:-1

ASIA

Asia is by far the largest and the most populous continent. It represents one-third of the world's land and holds nearly three-fifths of its people. Its terrain is tremendously varied, but is dominated by mountains, including the world's highest range, the Himalayas. Mountains, in fact, help to define the continent: The Ural Mountains separate Asia from Europe, which occupies the western part of Eurasia.

Asia is notable for its extremes. Mount Everest, on the Nepal-China border, is the world's highest mountain. The Tibetan Plateau is the world's largest and highest plateau. The shore of the salty Dead Sea, which lies between Israel and Jordan, is the lowest point on Earth. Lake Baikal in Siberia is the world's deepest lake.

India's Taj Mahal (above) was built to honor an emperor's wife; Japanese fans (left) are ornate works of art; the Great Wall of China (below) is the largest man-made structure in the world

Asia Facts

Area: 17,300,000 square miles (44,900,000 square kilometers)

Highest Mountain: Mount Everest, China-Nepal, 29,028 feet (8,848 meters)— *world's highest mountain*

Lowest Point: Dead Sea, Israel-Jordan, -1339 feet (-408 meters)—*world's lowest point*

Longest River: Yangtze, China, 3,900 miles (6,300 kilometers)

Largest Lake: Caspian Sea Asia/Europe, 143,240 square miles (370,990 square kilometers)

Largest Desert: Gobi, Mongolia-China, 500,000 square miles (1,295,000 square kilometers)

Largest Island: New Guinea Asia/Oceania, 309,000 square miles (800,000 square kilometers)

Land Elevation
Feet (Meters)

- 9,840 and over (3,000 and over)
- 6,560 - 9,840 (2,000 - 3,000)
- 3,280 - 6,560 (1,000 - 2,000)
- 1,640 - 3,280 (500 - 1,000)
- 656 - 1,640 (200 - 500)
- 0 - 656 feet (0 - 200)

ARCTIC OCEAN

SEVERNAYA ZEMLYA

NEW SIBERIAN ISLANDS

EAST SIBERIAN SEA

BERING SEA

KARA SEA

pol. Yamal

poluostrov Taymyr

LAPTEV SEA

Kolyma

poluostrov Kamchatka

Mys Lopatka

Noril'sk

Central Siberian Uplands

Arctic Circle

Indigirka

Lena

Verkhoyanskiy khrebet

SEA OF OKHOTSK

RUSSIA

West Siberian Lowland

S i b e r i a

Stanovoy khrebet

Amur

SAKHALIN

KURIL ISLANDS

Ob'

Yenisey

Angara

Tunguska

Lake Baikal

Tatar Strait

NOVOSIBIRSK

Ishim

Irtysh

Sayan Mts.

Selenga

Greater Khingan Range

Manchuria

Sikhote Alin

SEA OF JAPAN

HOKKAIDO

Ural Mountains

Ural

Kirghiz Steppe

KAZAKHSTAN

Aral Sea

Syr Darya

Lake Balkhash

Altai

MONGOLIA

HONSHŪ

JAPAN

TŌKYŌ

Caspian Sea

Ust-Urt Plateau

Kara Kum

TURKMENISTAN

UZBEKISTAN

KYRGYZSTAN

Tien Shan

Junggar Pendi

Gobi

BEIJING

NORTH KOREA

SOUTH KOREA

Mt. Fuji 12,388 Ft.

SHIKOKU

KYŪSHŪ

Korea Strait

Amu Darya

TAJIKISTAN

Pamir

Tarim Pendi

Qilian Shan

Kunlun Shan

Qaidam Pendi

Altun Shan

YELLOW SEA

EAST CHINA SEA

PACIFIC OCEAN

Elburz Mts.

Dasht-e Kavir

AFGHANISTAN

Hindu Kush

K2 28,250 Ft.

CHINA

Qin Ling

Huang

SHANGHAI

Dasht-e Lut

PAKISTAN

Plateau of Tibet

H i m a l a y a s

New Delhi

Yangtze

Wuyi Shan

Nan Ling

Tropic of Cancer

Gulf of Oman

Great Indian Desert

Indus

NEPAL

Mt. Everest 29,028 Ft.

BHUTAN

Ganges

Brahmaputra

TAIWAN

Taiwan Strait

Kāthiāwār Peninsula

INDIA

Godāvari

BANGLADESH

Irrawaddy

Salween

Mekong

Luzon Strait

LUZON

MUMBAI (BOMBAY)

D e c c a n

Western Ghats

Eastern Ghats

MYANMAR

LAOS

Red

Gulf of Tonkin

HAINAN DAO

Manila

PHILIPPINES

ARABIAN SEA

I n d o c h i n a

VIETNAM

MINDANAO

LAKSHADWEEP

Bay of Bengal

THAILAND

BANGKOK

CAMBODIA

SOUTH CHINA SEA

Cape Comorin

SRI LANKA

ANDAMAN ISLANDS

Andaman Sea

Gulf of Thailand

Mui Ca Mau

Sulu Sea

MALDIVES

NICOBAR ISLANDS

Malay Peninsula

BRUNEI

Celebes Sea

MOLUCCAS

NEW GUINEA

Equator

Str. of Malacca

MALAYSIA

CELEBES

CERAM

SINGAPORE

BORNEO

Banda Sea

Equator

SUMATRA

GREATER SUNDA ISLANDS

INDONESIA

TIMOR

INDIAN OCEAN

Java Sea

Jakarta

JAVA

Arafura Sea

Timor Sea

---

0   100   300   500 Miles

0   200   400   600   800 Kilometers

Scale 1:45,000,000; one inch to 710 miles

Copyright by Rand McNally & Co.
Made in U.S.A.
N-CMW60000-A1- -1-1-1

N
W   E
S

THE LAND

Only about a fifth of the continent is suitable for agriculture, but a large portion of Asia's people make their living off the land. In Asia's three most populous countries–China, India, and Russia–two-thirds of workers are farmers. Raising livestock is also an important job, especially in the central Asian grasslands. Given Asia's size, it is not surprising that the continent holds some of the world's largest reserves of oil, natural gas, and coal.

By building terraces that capture rainfall, farmers can grow rice on even the steepest hillsides.

Environments
Asia has a wide variety of environments, including large areas of arctic and subarctic tundra, broad deserts, heavy forests, and dry grasslands.

Environments

- Forest
- Swamp
- Crop and woodland
- Cropland
- Crop and grazing land
- Grassland
- Desert
- Tundra
- Barren
- Urban

Wood products are one of Indonesia's main exports.

Mineral Resources
In addition to its huge oil and coal reserves, Asia is also rich in metals such as iron ore, tin, lead, zinc, and bauxite. The continent furnishes raw materials for its own industries with plenty left over to export to the rest of the world.

Farming
Rice is Asia's most important crop: Asia produces 90 percent of the world's supply. Rice grows both in flooded fields called paddies and on terraced hillsides. With plentiful rainfall and fertile lowlands, countries such as India, Thailand, and China are the perfect places to grow rice–in fact, some areas grow three separate rice crops each year.

Forestry
In chilly Siberia, forests cover more than one-third of the land. In southeast Asia, the exotic hardwoods in the rain forests are used mainly for making furniture. Unfortunately, the trees are being cut down faster than they can grow back, and entire Asian forests are in danger of disappearing.

Tourism
Tourism is an important source of income for many Asian countries. The continent offers a broad range of travel destinations, including the Taj Mahal, China's Great Wall, Mount Everest and other high Himalayan peaks, the ancient temples of Myanmar, and holy sites of the Middle East.

Economies

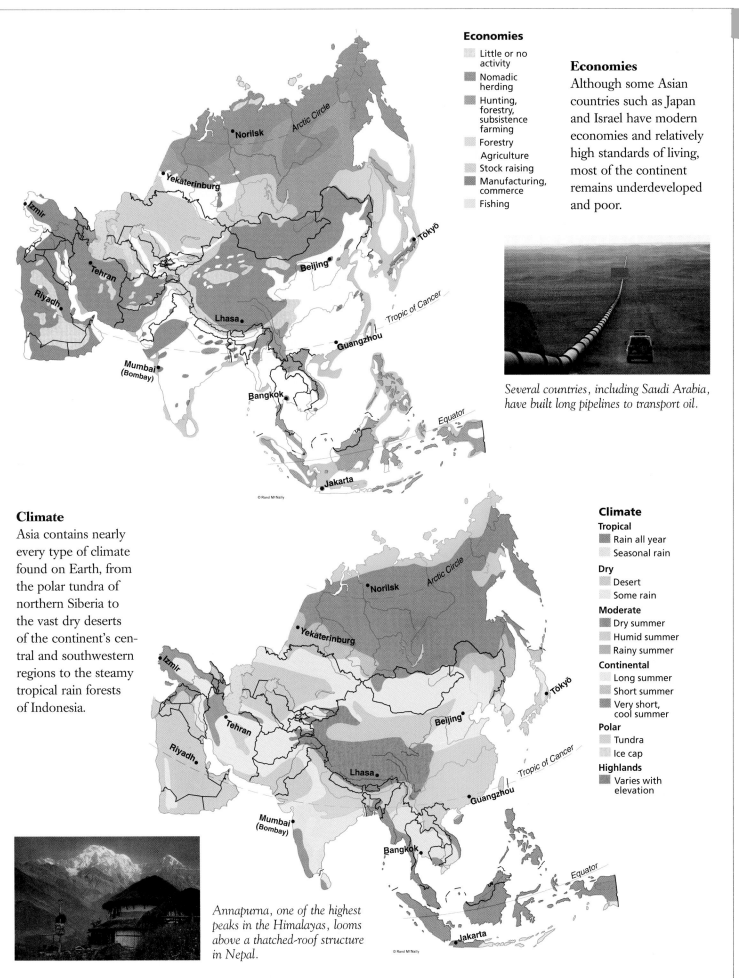

Economies

Little or no activity

Nomadic herding

Hunting, forestry, subsistence farming

Forestry

Agriculture

Stock raising

Manufacturing, commerce

Fishing

Economies

Although some Asian countries such as Japan and Israel have modern economies and relatively high standards of living, most of the continent remains underdeveloped and poor.

Several countries, including Saudi Arabia, have built long pipelines to transport oil.

Climate

Asia contains nearly every type of climate found on Earth, from the polar tundra of northern Siberia to the vast dry deserts of the continent's central and southwestern regions to the steamy tropical rain forests of Indonesia.

Climate

Tropical

Rain all year

Seasonal rain

Dry

Desert

Some rain

Moderate

Dry summer

Humid summer

Rainy summer

Continental

Long summer

Short summer

Very short, cool summer

Polar

Tundra

Ice cap

Highlands

Varies with elevation

Annapurna, one of the highest peaks in the Himalayas, looms above a thatched-roof structure in Nepal.

THE PEOPLE

Asia is the most culturally and ethnically diverse continent, mainly due to its enormous size. Three out of every five people on Earth live in Asia. While many Asians are farmers and live in the countryside or in small villages, the continent's cities are among the world's largest and most crowded. Tokyo, Japan, is the most populous metropolitan area on Earth. China, with more than one billion people, is the world's most populous country.

Sleds drawn by reindeer help Siberians travel across the deep snow.

Chinese children perform at a festival.

In India, a merchant keeps track of business transactions in a ledger.

As part of their Islamic faith, Muslims observe the holy month of Ramadan.

Buddhist monks gather outside a temple in Bangkok, Thailand.

A young herder tends sheep and cattle in the mountains of Uzbekistan.

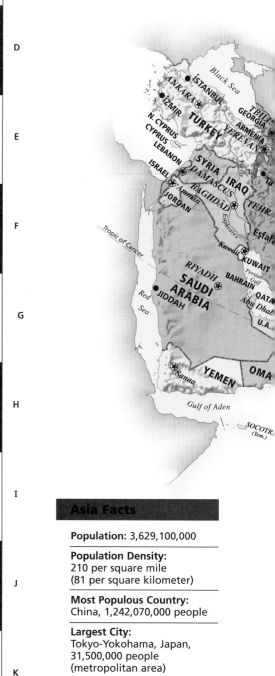

Asia Facts

Population: 3,629,100,000

Population Density:
210 per square mile
(81 per square kilometer)

Most Populous Country:
China, 1,242,070,000 people

Largest City:
Tokyo-Yokohama, Japan,
31,500,000 people
(metropolitan area)

4 5 6 7 8 9 10 11

ARCTIC OCEAN

SEVERNAYA
ZEMLYA

NEW SIBERIAN
ISLANDS

EAST SIBERIAN
SEA

BERING
SEA

KARA SEA

LAPTEV
SEA

Arctic Circle

Norilsk

Yana

Indigirka

Lena

Yakutsk

Magadan

Poliustrov
Kamchatka
Petropavlovsk-
Kamchatskiy

SEA OF
OKHOTSK

SAKHALIN

KURIL ISLANDS

India's Ganges River is
sacred to Hindus, who
believe that bathing in its
waters will wash away
their sins.

YEKATERINBURG

CHELYABINSK

Tyumen

Ob' Surgut

Ishim

Irtysh

R U S S I A

Angara

Yenisey

Krasnoyarsk

Lake
Baikal

Amur

Khabarovsk

Tatar Strait

SAPPORO

HOKKAIDŌ

OMSK

NOVOSIBIRSK

Barnaul

Irkutsk

Chita

QIQIHAR

HARBIN

Vladivostok

SEA OF
JAPAN

HONSHŪ
JAPAN
TŌKYŌ

Astana
(Aqmola)
Qaraghandy

Semey

Selenge

Ulan Bator

MONGOLIA

CHANGCHUN

SHENYANG

NORTH
KOREA
P'YONGYANG JAPAN

NAGOYA

KAZAKHSTAN

Aral
Sea

Syr Darya

Lake
Balkhash

Bishkek

ALMATY

ÜRÜMQI

BEIJING TIANJIN

SEOUL
SOUTH
KOREA OSAKA

SHIKOKU
KYUSHŪ

BAKU

TASHKENT

UZBEKISTAN

TURKMENISTAN

KYRGYZSTAN

TAIYUAN

JINAN

YELLOW
SEA

PUSAN

Ashgabat

TAJIKISTAN
Dushanbe

LANZHOU

C H I N A

XI'AN

NANJING

SHANGHAI

HANGZHOU

EAST
CHINA SEA

PACIFIC OCEAN

MASHHAD

KABUL

AFGHANISTAN

Amu Darya

WUHAN

Huang

Tropic of Cancer

Islāmābād

CHENGDU

CHONGQING

Fuzhou

T'AIPEI

TAIWAN

KAOHSIUNG

PAKISTAN

LAHORE

DELHI

Lhasa

Yangtze

Taiwan Strait

KARĀCHI

Gulf of Oman

New
Delhi

KĀNPUR

NEPAL
Kathmandu
Thimphu
BHUTAN

Ganges

Brahmaputra

KUNMING

GUANGZHOU

HONG
KONG

Luzon Strait

Muscat

AHMADĀBĀD

INDIA

BANGLA-
DESH DHAKA

Chittagong

Ha Noi

Gulf of
Tonkin

LUZON

MANILA

PHILIPPINES

ARABIAN
SEA

MUMBAI
(BOMBAY)

CALCUTTA

NĀGPUR

Godāvari

MYANMAR
(BURMA)

LAOS

Viangchan

Mekong

HAINAN DAO

Da Nang

Cebu

PUNE

HYDERĀBĀD

YANGON

THAILAND

VIETNAM

SOUTH

MINDANAO

Davao

Young people in
Turkey show off
colorful traditional
clothing.

BANGALORE

CHENNAI
(MADRAS)

Bay of
Bengal

BANGKOK

CAMBODIA
Phnum
Penh

CHINA

SEA

Sulu Sea

SRI LANKA

ANDAMAN
ISLANDS
(India)

Gulf of
Thailand

THANH PHO
HO CHI MINH

Equator

MALDIVES Male'

Colombo

NICOBAR
ISLANDS
(India)

Str. of Malacca

Malay
Peninsula

Bandar Seri
Begawan

BRUNEI

Celebes Sea

Manado

NEW GUINEA

MEDAN

Kuala
Lumpur

MALAYSIA

BORNEO

CELEBES

CERAM

Banda Sea

Arafura Sea

INDIAN OCEAN

Equator

SINGAPORE

SUMATRA

PALEMBANG

Java Sea

I N D O N E S I A

Banjarmasin

TIMOR

Timor Sea

JAKARTA
BANDUNG JAVA

SURABAYA

0 200 400 600 800 1000 Miles

0 300 600 900 1200 1500 Kilometers

N
W   E
S

Scale 1:45,000,000; one inch to 710 miles
Copyright by Rand McNally & Co.
Made in U.S.A.
N-CMW60000-P1- -1-1-1

SOUTHWEST ASIA

Southwest Asia borders Europe—in fact, a small part of Turkey actually falls within Europe. Turkey's most fertile farmlands spread along its lengthy coast, although wheat and barley grow in the dry plateau area in the center of the country. Armenia, Azerbaijan, and Georgia, which all lie in the mountainous region between the Black Sea and the Caspian Sea, possess abundant mineral wealth.

Grapes ripen on vines in the rugged Troodos Mountains, which dominate the center of the island of Cyprus.

A Turkish farmer rides a donkey across a wheat field.

Sheep graze near an ancient Roman temple in western Armenia.

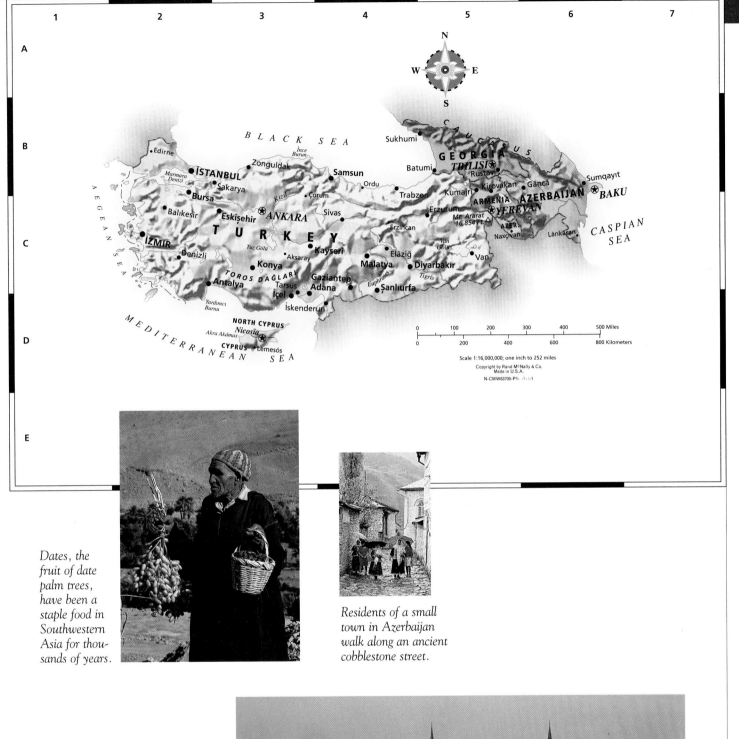

Dates, the fruit of date palm trees, have been a staple food in Southwestern Asia for thousands of years.

Residents of a small town in Azerbaijan walk along an ancient cobblestone street.

Istanbul's magnificent Church of Hagia Sofia rises above the Bosporus Strait, which separates Asia and Europe.

RUSSIA AND CENTRAL ASIA

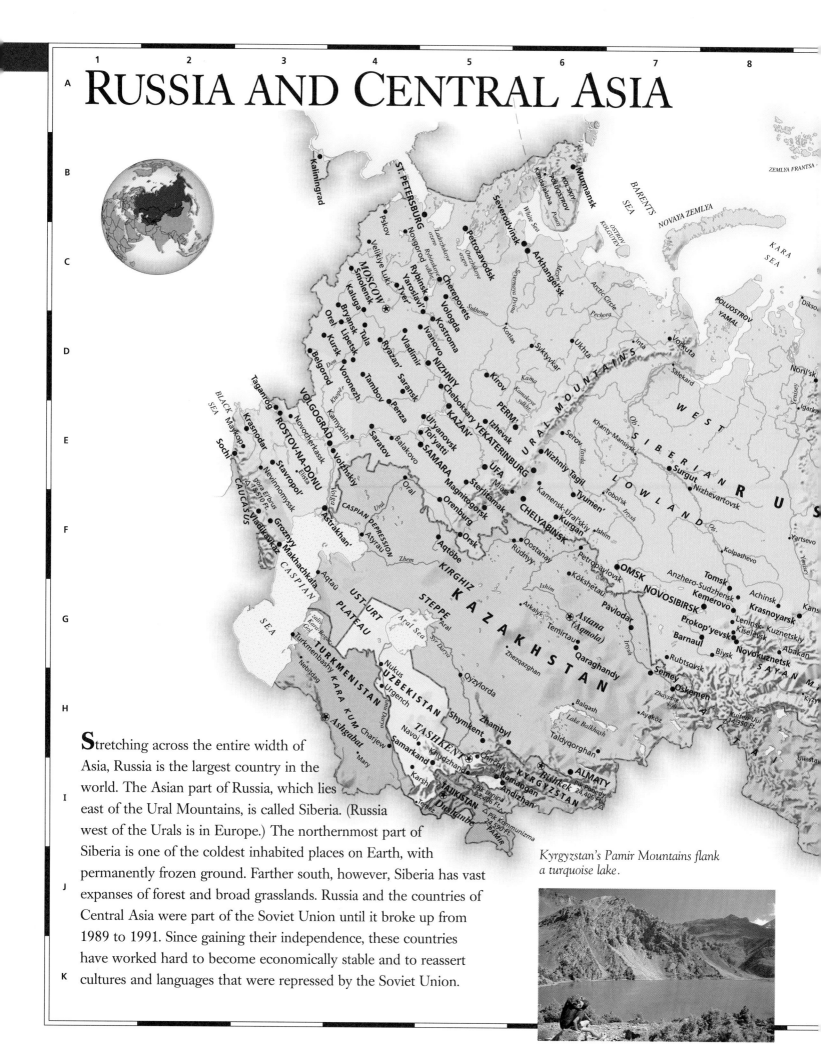

Stretching across the entire width of Asia, Russia is the largest country in the world. The Asian part of Russia, which lies east of the Ural Mountains, is called Siberia. (Russia west of the Urals is in Europe.) The northernmost part of Siberia is one of the coldest inhabited places on Earth, with permanently frozen ground. Farther south, however, Siberia has vast expanses of forest and broad grasslands. Russia and the countries of Central Asia were part of the Soviet Union until it broke up from 1989 to 1991. Since gaining their independence, these countries have worked hard to become economically stable and to reassert cultures and languages that were repressed by the Soviet Union.

Kyrgyzstan's Pamir Mountains flank a turquoise lake.

Many people in Central Asia live in yurts—circular tents covered with animal hides.

The train station at Vladivostok, Russia, marks the eastern end of the Trans-Siberian Railroad. The route begins in Moscow and runs 5,800 miles (9,280 kilometers) through Russia.

Cotton, one of Central Asia's main cash crops, is grown on flat grasslands known as "steppes."

A man in Uzbekistan engraves ornate patterns into decorative plates.

Siberian tigers can withstand the brutal cold of northern winters.

Scale 1:24,000,000; one inch to 379 miles
Copyright by Rand McNally & Co.
Made in U.S.A.
N-CMW60091-P1- -1- l-1

EAST ASIA

Tokyo, Japan, is the most populous city in the world.

China, the most populous country in the world and the third-largest in land area, dominates East Asia. Much of western China's landscape is harsh and barren, encompassing the high, rugged Tibetan Plateau and two vast deserts, the Gobi and the Takla Makan. Most of China's people live in the eastern part of the country, where there are fertile plains, river valleys, and deltas. Japan is a mountainous island country. Although little of its land is suitable for farming, rice grows in lowland areas and on terraced hillsides. Despite having few natural resources, Japan has become one of the world's wealthiest and most highly industrialized countries.

South Korea and North Korea occupy a peninsula east of China. Once a single, united country, Korea was divided into North and South Korea following World War II. South Korea has most of the farmland, while North Korea is highly industrialized.

ALTAI

JUNGGAR PENDI

Yining
Manas
ÜRÜMQI
TIEN SHAN
Pik Pobedy 24,406 Ft.
Kashi
Aksu
Hami
Shache
BEI SHAN
TARIM PENDI
Hotan
G
Yumen
ALTUN SHAN
QILIAN SHAN
K2 28,250 Ft.
Zhangye
KUNLUN SHAN
Muztag 25,338 Ft.
QAIDAM PENDI
Wuwei
Golmud
Qinghai Hu
Bangong Co
Xining
PLATEAU
Yagradagzê Shan 17,854 Ft.
A'NYÊMAQÊN SHAN
LANZHOU
Leli Shan 21,020 Ft.
OF TIBET
Huang
Kangrinboqê Feng 22,028 Ft.
Tia
GANGDISÊ SHAN
Nam Co
BAYAN HAR SHAN
CHINA
HIMALAYAS
Salween
Guang
Xigazê
Lhasa
Brahmaputra
Namjagbarwa Feng 25,446 Ft.
Guanxian Nanc
Mt. Everest 29,028 Ft.
CHENGDU
Suini
Gongga Shan 24,790 Ft.
Yangtze
Wutongqiao
Zig
Xichang
Yi
Zhaotong
Ansh
KUNMING
Baoshan
Tropic of Cancer
Tonghai
Wenshan
Gejiu

With an excellent natural harbor, Kaosiung is the fastest-growing city in Taiwan.

Kabuki Theater in Japan dates back to the early 1600s.

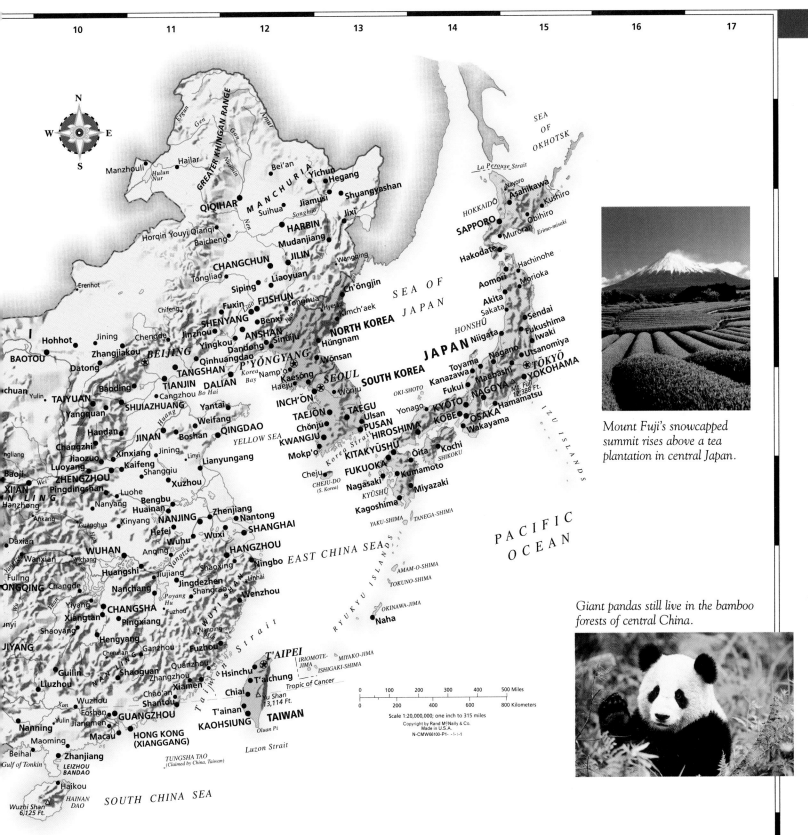

N
W E
S

10   11   12   13   14   15   16   17

GREATER KHINGAN RANGE
Ergun
Gen
Amur
Gan
Nonni
Manzhouli
Hailar
Hulun
Nur
Bei'an
Yichun
Hegang
MANCHURIA
Shuangyashan
QIQIHAR
Suihua
Jiamusi
Songhua
Jixi
HARBIN
Nen
Mudanjiang
Horqin Youyi Qianqi
Baicheng
Wangqing
CHANGCHUN
JILIN
Erenhot
Tongliao
Liaoyuan
Chifeng
Siping
Ch'ŏngjin
Hohhot
Jining
Chengde
Fuxin
FUSHUN
Tonghua
Kimch'aek
Liao
Yalu
Hyesan
BAOTOU
Zhangjiakou
BEIJING
Jinzhou
SHENYANG
Benxi
Sinŭiju
NORTH KOREA
Hŭngnam
Datong
Yingkou
Dandong
P'YŎNGYANG
Wŏnsan
chuan
Yulin
TANGSHAN
Qinhuangdao
Namp'o
Kaesŏng
SEOUL
SOUTH KOREA
Baoding
TIANJIN
DALIAN
Korea
Bay
Haeju
INCH'ŎN
TAIYUAN
Cangzhou
Bo Hai
SHIJIAZHUANG
Yantai
Yangquan
Weifang
QINGDAO
TAEJŎN
TAEGU
Ulsan
Handan
JINAN
Boshan
YELLOW SEA
Chŏnju
PUSAN
Changzhi
Xinxiang
Jining
KWANGJU
HIROSHIMA
Jiaozuo
Kaifeng
Linyi
Lianyungang
Mokp'o
KITAKYŪSHŪ
Luoyang
Shangqiu
Cheju
FUKUOKA
Baoji
ZHENGZHOU
Xuzhou
CHEJU-DO
(S. Korea)
Nagasaki
KYŪSHŪ
XI'AN
Pingdingshan
Wei
Luohe
Nanyang
Bengbu
Huainan
Hanzhong
Xinyang
NANJING
Zhenjiang
Nantong
Ankang
Hefei
SHANGHAI
Daxian
Wuhu
Wuxi
Anqing
HANGZHOU
Yichang
WUHAN
Yangtze
Ningbo
EAST CHINA SEA
Huangshi
Jiujiang
Shaoxing
ONGQING
Changde
Nanchang
Jingdezhen
Wenzhou
Yiyang
Poyang
Hu
Shangrao
XIANGTAN
CHANGSHA
Fuzhou
JIYANG
Pingxiang
Shaoyang
Hengyang
Ganzhou
Fuzhou
unyi
Guilin
Shaoguan
Liuzhou
Zhangzhou
Xiamen
Wuzhou
Cháo'an
Chiai
Nanning
Foshan
Shantou
Maoming
Jiangmen
GUANGZHOU
Macau
HONG KONG
(XIANGGANG)
Beihai
Zhanjiang
Gulf of Tonkin
LEIZHOU
BANDAO
Haikou
HAINAN
DAO
Wuzhi Shan
6,125 Ft.
SOUTH CHINA SEA

SEA OF OKHOTSK
La Perouse Strait
Nayoro
Asahikawa
Kushiro
HOKKAIDŌ
SAPPORO
Obihiro
Muroran
Erimo-misaki
Hakodate
Hachinohe
Aomori
Morioka
Akita
Sakata
Sendai
HONSHŪ
Niigata
Fukushima
Iwaki
Nagano
Utsunomiya
Toyama
TŌKYŌ
Kanazawa
Maebashi
YOKOHAMA
Fukui
NAGOYA
Mt. Fuji
12,388 Ft.
KYOTO
Hamamatsu
KOBE
OSAKA
IZU ISLANDS
Yonago
Wakayama
OKI-SHOTO
Oita
Kochi
SHIKOKU
Kumamoto
Miyazaki
Kagoshima
YAKU-SHIMA
TANEGA-SHIMA
PACIFIC
OCEAN
RYUKYU ISLANDS
AMAM-O-SHIMA
TOKUNO-SHIMA
OKINAWA-JIMA
Naha

SEA OF JAPAN
JAPAN

T'AIPEI
Hsinchu
IRIOMOTE-JIMA
MIYAKO-JIMA
ISHIGAKI-SHIMA
T'aichung
Tropic of Cancer
Chiai
Yu Shan
13,114 Ft.
T'ainan
TAIWAN
KAOHSIUNG
Oluan Pi
Luzon Strait
TUNGSHA TAO
(Claimed by China, Taiwan)

| 0 | 100 | 200 | 300 | 400 | 500 Miles |
| 0 | 200 | 400 | 600 | 800 Kilometers |

Scale 1:20,000,000; one inch to 315 miles
Copyright by Rand McNally & Co.
Made in U.S.A.
N-CMW66100-P1- -!- !-1

Mount Fuji's snowcapped summit rises above a tea plantation in central Japan.

Giant pandas still live in the bamboo forests of central China.

Bicycles are a popular way to travel through the crowded streets of Chinese cities.

Almost all of the world's large-scale silk production takes place in Asia, where shops like this one in South Korea display hundreds of brightly-colored fabric bolts.

SOUTHEAST ASIA

Hot, humid Southeast Asia consists of an enormous peninsula–known as Indochina–and some 20,000 islands. Rice is the major crop, but other tropical crops grow here, too. Palm oil from Malaysia, rubber from Indonesia, coconuts and sugarcane from the Philippines, and hardwoods from throughout the region contribute significantly to the regional economy. Mineral resources, including oil, coal, natural gas, and tin, are also abundant. In fact, oil and natural gas reserves in Brunei have made this small country one of the world's richest. In recent years, tiny Singapore has become an important international center of business and finance.

Thailand's long coast is lined with many secluded inlets, like this one near Phuket.

Bicycles are the best way for fruit vendors in Hanoi, Vietnam, to distribute their produce.

Tropic of Cancer

PATKAI RANGE
Chindwin
Nmai
Mali

Myitkyinā

Bhamo

CHIN HILLS

Monywa   **Mandalay**
Mt. Victoria   Maymyo
10,016 Ft. △   Pakokku
Chauk   **MYANMAR**
Meiktila   Taunggyi
Yenangyaung   Chiang Rai
Sittwe   **(BURMA)**

Phan Si Pang
10,312 Ft.
Phôngsali
Ha Noi
Hoa Binh   Hong Gai
Hai Phong
Nam Dinh
Louangphrabang
Thanh Hoa
Gulf of Tonkin
Vinh

ARAKAN YOMA

Prome   Toungoo
Chiang Mai   Lampang
Doi Inthanon △
8,530 Ft.
Henzada

YANGON   Bago
Thaton
Pathein
Pagoda
Point   *Gulf of
Martaban*
Mawlamyine

Phou Bia
9,249 Ft. △
LAOS
Viangchan

VIETNAM
Dong Hoi

Uttaradit
Nong Khai   Udon Thani
Phitsanulok
THAILAND   Khon Kaen   Savannakhét
Nakhon Sawan   Kalasin
Takhli   Ubon Ratchathani
Nakhon Ratchasima
Saraburi
Phra Nakhon Si Ayutthaya
Dawei

Hue
Da Nang

Ngoc Linh
8,524 Ft.
△   Quang Ngai
• Kon Tum
• Play Cu
Qui Nhon
Tuy Hoa
• Buon Me Thuot

*THIU KHAO
PHANOM DONGRAK*

BANGKOK
Chon Buri
Rayong   Bâtdâmbâng
Bang Tônlé   Mekong
Hua Hin   Chanthaburi   Sab
Mergui

Andaman Sea

CAMBODIA
Kâmpóng
Cham   Da Lat
*Gulf of
Thailand*
Phnum Aôral
5,948 Ft. △
Phnum Pénh
Bien
Hoa
Kâmpóng Saôm
Phan Thiet
My   **THANH PHO HO CHI MINH**
Tho
Long Xuyen   Can Tho   Vung Tau
Rach Gia   Soc Trang
Ca Mau

**ISTHMUS
OF KRA**

Mui Ca Mau

Surat Thani
Nakhon Si Thammarat

Thung Song
• Phuket
Trang   Phatthalung
Songkhla
Hat Yai
Kanger   Yala
Narathiwat
Alor Setar
Great Channel   **Kota Bharu**
Banda Aceh   George Town   Kuala Terengganu
Butterworth
Gunung Abongatong △   Taiping   Dungan
9,793 Ft.   **Ipoh**   Gunong Tahan
7,175 Ft. △
Binjai   **MEDAN**   **MALAYSIA**
Kuala Lumpur   Kuantan
Tebingtinggi   Tanjungbalai   Pahang
Pematangsiantar   Kelang
Dayan   Seremban
Toba   Melaka
PALAU SIMEULUE   Muar   Keluang
Sibolga   Dumai   Johor Bahru
Padangsidempuan   **SINGAPORE** ✪ **SINGAPORE**
PALAU NIAS   Tanjungpinang
Pekanbaru

Strait of Malacca

PARACEL ISLAN
(Claimed By China, T
and Vietnam)

SPRATLY ISLA

*KEPULAUAN
NATUNA
BESAR*

Binjai

*KEPULAUAN
ANAMBAS*

Tanjung Datu
Sibu
MALAY
Kuching
Gunung Niut
5,581 Ft. △
Singkawang

Equator

Bukittinggi   Tembilahan
SUMATRA
Padang
△Gunung Kerinci   **Jambi**
12,467 Ft.
PALAU SIBERUT   *PULAU BANGKA*
Pangkalpinang
Hari
BELITUNG
Tanjungpandan
Musi   **PALEMBANG**
• Perabumulih
Lahat
Bengkulu   Gunung Dempo
10,364 Ft.
Kotabumi
**Bandar
Lampung**

Pontianak
Kapuas
Palangkar

Tanjung Jabung
*Tanjung
Sambar*   *Tanjung Puting*
Tanjung Lumut

I   **N**   *JAVA SE*

Tanjung Cina
JAKARTA   Karawang   *GREATER S*
Bogor   Cirebon
Cianjur   Kudus   MAD
BANDUNG   **SEMARANG**   **SURABA**
Garut   Magelang
Purwokerto   **Surakarta**
JAVA   **Yogyakarta**   Mal

INDIAN OCEAN

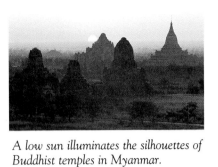

A family of
monkeys sits
in front of a
temple in
Myanmar.

A low sun illuminates the silhouettes of
Buddhist temples in Myanmar.

Luzon Strait

BABUYAN ISLANDS

Mayraira Point

Escarpada Point

Laoag

Vigan

Ilagan

San Fernando

LUZON

Baguio

SIERRA MADRE

Dagupan

Tarlac

Cabanatuan

Angeles

PHILIPPINE

SEA

MANILA ⊛ ● Quezon City

Laguna de Bay

Lucena ● Naga

Legaspi

S O U T H

CHINA SEA

MINDORO

Bohol Sea

SAMAR

Libro Point

PHILIPPINES

Tacloban

PANAY

LEYTE

Iloilo ● **Bacolod**

Cebu

PALAWAN

Tagbilaran

Puerto Princesa

NEGROS

Dumaguete

Sibuyan Sea

● Butuan

SULU SEA

● **Cagayan de Oro**

Pagadian ● Marawi ● Bislig

Balabac Strait

MINDANAO

Davao

P A C I F I C

Zamboanga ● Cotabato

Mount Apo 9,692 Ft. *Cape San Agustin*

O C E A N

Koronadal ● **General Santos**

Gunong Kinabalu 13,455 Ft.

Sandakan

Jolo

Tinaca Point

ota Kinabalu

Tanjong Hog

KEPULAUAN TALAUD

NEI

Bandar Seri Begawan

Tawau

Pagon 070 Ft.

Tarakan

CELEBES SEA

Kuala Lumpur began as a small
mining settlement, but today it
is the bustling capital of Malaysia.

MOROTAI

Tanjung Kandi

Manado △ Gunung Klabat 6,634 Ft.

HALMAHERA

Tanjung Mangkalihat

△ Bukit Malino 8,015 Ft. ● Gorontalo

Equator

Samarinda

Teluk Tomini

MOLUCCA Sea

Sorong

JAZIRAH DOBERAI

Tanjung D'Urville

ORNEO

Balikapan

Palu

Tanjung Api

Tanjung Libobo

KEPULAUAN OBI

PULAU MISOOL

Teluk Cenderawasih

Jayapura

Tanjung Aru

CELEBES

Danau Poso

KEPULAUAN SULU

CERAM Sea

SEMENANJUNG BOMBERAI

PEGUNUNGAN MAOKE

Banjarmasin

Bulu Rantekombola 11,335 Ft. △

Danau Towuti

BURU

CERAM

● Ambon

Puncak Jaya 16,503 Ft.

Puncak Trikora 15,584 Ft.

Martapura

Parepare ●

Tanjung Selatan

Singkang ● MOLUCCAS

Watampone

Kendari

I

A

Puncak Mandala 15,617 Ft.

O N E S

Tual ●

NEW GUINEA

Ujungpandang

KEPULAUAN ARU

Tanjung De Jongs

Digul

DA ISLANDS

BANDA SEA

KEPULAUAN BARAT DAYA

PULAU YAMDENA

PULAU YOS SUDARSO

Tanjung Vals

Bali Sea

BALI

Gunung Rinjani 12,224 Ft.

Gunung Tambora 9,350 Ft.

Flores Sea

Mataram

Raba

FLORES

Ende

pasar

LOMBOK SUMBAWA

Memboro

Tanjung Sasar

LESSER SUNDA ISLANDS

TIMOR

Timor Sea

ARAFURA SEA

SUMBA

Kupang

0 100 200 300 400 500 Miles

0 200 400 600 800 Kilometers

Scale 1:16,000,000; one inch to 252 miles

Copyright by Rand McNally & Co.
Made in U.S.A.

Two cattle pull a farmer
through a rice paddy in
Bali, Indonesia.

Elementary schoolchildren play in Zamboanga, on
the Philippine island of Mindanao.

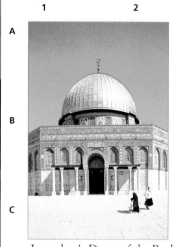

Jerusalem's Dome of the Rock is an important Muslim shrine.

Saudi Arabia's Ar Rub' al Khāli, or "The Empty Quarter," contains mountainous sand ridges.

MEDITERRANEAN SEA

Caspian Sea

Al-Qāmishlī
Khvoy
Marand
Ahar
Orūmīyeh
Tabrīz
Ardabīl
HALAB
Idlib
Ar Raqqah
Al Mawşil
Irbīl
Lake Urmia
Marāgheh
Maneh
Rasht
Al Lādhiqīyah
Ţarābulus
Tartūs
Hamāh
Dayr az Zawr
As Sulaymānāyah
Karkūk
Mahābād
Zanjān
Sārī
Gonbad-e Qābūs
Qūchān
MASHI
Ḩimş
Dayr
Euphrates
Sanandaj
Qazvīn
Karaj
Āmol
ELBURZ MTS.
Sabzevār
Neyshābūr
LEBANON
Saydā
Beirut
SYRIA
Tigris
TEHRĀN
Qolleh-ye Damāvand 18,386 Ft.
Torbat-e Heydarīyeh
Her
Haifa
DAMASCUS
BAGHDĀD
Bākhtarān
Dez
Hamadān
Qom
IRAN
DASHT-E KAVĪR
Teverya
Irbid
Ar Ramādī
Borūjerd
Arāk
Kāshān
Birjand
ISRAEL
Tel Aviv-Yafo
Az-Zarqā'
Amman
IRAQ
Al Hillah
Khorramābād
Najafābād
Eşfahān
Ardakān
Gaza
Jerusalem
Dozful
Masjed-e Soleymān
Qomsheh
Yazd
DASHT-E LUT
Be'er Sheva
Dead Sea
JORDAN
An Najaf
Al 'Amārah
Ahvāz
Abādān
Hawr al-Hammar
Zābol
Jabal Ramm 5,755 Ft.
An Nāşirīyah
Basra
Daryācheh-ye Hamūn
Jabal Al Lawz 7,884 Ft.
Gulf of 'Aqaba
Tabūk
AN NAFŪD
KUWAIT
BŪBIYĀN
Al Jahrah
Kuwait
Kermān
Zāhedān
Ra's Abu Madd
Hā'il
Bam
AL-HIJĀZ
Buraydah
Persian Gulf
Bandar-e Būshehr
Jahrom
Shīrāz
ZAGROS MTS.
RED SEA
SAUDI ARABIA
Medina
Ad Dammām
BAHRAIN
Al Khubar
Al Manāmah
QATAR
AD DAHNĀ
Al Hufūf
Ad Dawḩah
Ash Shariqah
Bandar-e 'Abbās
Strait of Hormuz
JAZĪREH-YE QESHM
OMAN
Gulf of Oman
JIDDAH
Mecca
At Ta'if
RIYADH
ARABIAN PENINSULA
Dubayy
Abu Dhabi
Al 'Ayn
Muscat
UNITED ARAB EMIRATES
Jabal ash-Shām 9,957 Ft.
Sūr
Ra's al Yadd
Jabal Sawdā' 10,522 Ft.
AR RUB' AL KHĀLI
OMAN
MAŞĪRAH
Abha
Khamis Mushayt
Khalīj Maşīrah
Abā as Su'ūd
Ra's al Madrakha
Dawḩat Şawqirah
Şa'dah
Şalālah
an-Nabī Shu'ayb Jabal 12,008 Ft.
Sanaa
Ghubbat al Qamar
Ra's Fartak
Al Hudaydah
YEMEN
Ta'izz
Al Mukallā
Aden
Bab el Mandeb
Gulf of Aden
SOCOTRA (Yemen)

INDIAN

SOUTH ASIA AND THE MIDDLE EAST

South Asia is separated from the rest of Asia by the highest mountains in the world: the Himalayas, the Karakoram Range and the Hindu Kush. Nepal and Bhutan lie tilted along the southern slopes of the Himalayas, their land rising steeply from low plains and foothills up to the loftiest mountaintops. To the south is India, the second-most populous country in the world, after China. To the west of South Asia is the Middle East. Deserts cover much of this region, but beneath the desert sands lies a fortune in oil and natural gas. These resources have made many Middle Eastern countries wealthy, but have also sparked conflict in the region.

Soldiers enjoy a meal in Afghanistan.

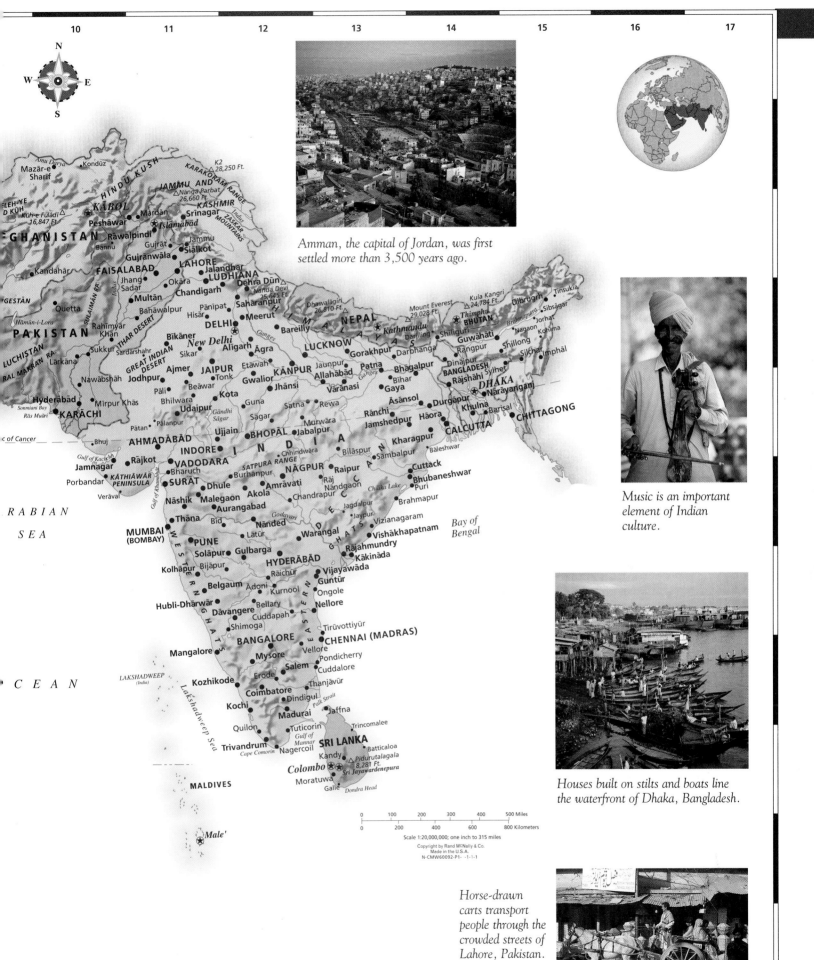

10   11   12   13   14   15   16   17

Amman, the capital of Jordan, was first
settled more than 3,500 years ago.

Music is an important
element of Indian
culture.

Houses built on stilts and boats line
the waterfront of Dhaka, Bangladesh.

Horse-drawn
carts transport
people through the
crowded streets of
Lahore, Pakistan.

Scale 1:20,000,000; one inch to 315 miles
Copyright by Rand McNally & Co.
Made in the U.S.A.
N-CMW60092-P1- -1-1-1

0   100   200   300   400   500 Miles
0   200   400   600   800 Kilometers

AUSTRALIA
& OCEANIA

Australia & Oceania Facts

Area: 3,300,000 square miles (8,500,000 square kilometers)

Highest Mountain: Mount Wilhelm, Papua New Guinea, 14,793 feet (4,509 meters)

Lowest Point: Lake Eyre, Australia, -52 feet (-16 meters)

Longest River: Murray River, 1,566 miles (2,520 kilometers)

Largest Lake: Lake Eyre, Australia, 3,430 square miles (8,884 square kilometers)

Largest Desert: Great Victorian Desert, Australia, 200,000 square miles (518,000 square kilometers)

Largest Island: New Guinea, Oceania/Asia, 308,882 square miles (799,696 square kilometers)

ARAFURA

TIMOR SEA

MELVILLE ISLAND

Cape Croker · Cobourg Peninsula

Darwin ★

Arnhem Land

Cape Londonderry

Joseph Bonaparte Gulf

Daly

Victoria

Barkly Ta

INDIAN OCEAN

Cape Leveque

Mt. Hann 2,556 Ft.

Mt. Ord 3,074 Ft.

Kimberley Plateau

King Leopold Ranges

Fitzroy

NORTHERN

Tanami Desert

TERRITORY

Eighty Mile Beach

Great Sandy Desert

A U S T R A L I

Lake Auld

Mt. Leisier 2,943 Ft.

Mt. Liebig 5,000 Ft.

Mt. Zeil 4,957 Ft.

MacDonnell Ranges

North West Cape

Mt. Brockman 3,714 Ft.

Mt. Bruce 4,052 Ft.

Hamersley Range

Mt. Meharry 4,104 Ft.

Gibson Desert

Mt. Aloysius 3,560 Ft.

Lake Amadeus

Ayers Rock 2,844 Ft.

Mt. Cockburn 3,734 Ft.

Mt. Woodroffe 4,724 Ft.

Mt. Augustus 3,625 Ft.

WESTERN

Lake Carnegie

Tropic of Capricorn

Shark Bay

DIRK HARTOG ISLAND

AUSTRALIA

Great Victoria Desert

SOUTH AUSTRA

Nullarbor Plain

Gair

Great Australian Bight

Darling Range

Perth ★

Geographe Bay

Bluff Knoll 3,596 Ft.

Cape Naturaliste

Hood Point

Cape Arid

ARCHIPELAGO OF THE RECHERCHE

We

Cape Leeuwin Point D'Entrecasteaux

INDIAN OCEAN

Australia's Aborigines believe that Ayers Rock (above) is sacred; Sydney, Australia (below), is built around one of the world's largest natural harbors.

"**A**ustralia" has two meanings. It is the name of both the world's smallest, flattest continent and the world's sixth-largest country, which occupies the entire continent. It is the only inhabited continent that lies completely within the southern hemisphere; for this reason it has been nicknamed "The Land Down Under." Most of Australia's interior–the Outback–is barren desert, sparsely populated but ruggedly beautiful, with dramatic landforms such as Ayers Rock. Australia's best-known geographic feature, however, is the Great Barrier Reef, Earth's largest living structure, which stretches 1,250 miles (2,000 kilometers) through the Coral Sea off Australia's eastern coast.

To the north and east of Australia lies Oceania, which is made up of more than 25,000 volcanic islands and coral atolls scattered across the Pacific Ocean. A few of the islands, such as New Guinea and New Zealand's North and South Islands, are relatively large, but many others are too small to appear on any but the most detailed maps.

Torres Strait
Cape York
Cape York Peninsula
CORAL SEA
Gulf of Carpentaria
Bartle Frere 5,322 Ft.
△
Great Barrier Reef
Halifax Bay
Gregory Range
Great Dividing Range
Clarke Range
△ Mt. Dalrymple 4,131 Ft.
Selwyn Range
Great Artesian Basin
QUEENSLAND
Cape Capricorn
Tropic of Capricorn
Sandy Cape
FRASER ISLAND
PACIFIC
OCEAN
Impson Desert
Mt. Kiangarow 3,760 Ft. △
Cooper Creek
Darling Downs
Brisbane
● Southport
Cape Byron
Sturt Stony Desert
Grey Range
Barwon
Lake Eyre North
Darling
Lake Torrens
Barrier Range
NORFOLK ISLAND
Mary Peak 3,871 Ft. △
NEW SOUTH WALES
Murray
Lachlan
Darling
Penrith
Newcastle
Sydney
Great Dividing Range
Wollongong
Adelaide ★
Encounter Bay
NGAROO ISLAND
Canberra A.C.T. ⊛
Jervis Bay
Snowy Mts. △ Mt. Kosciuszko 7,313 Ft.
Cape Jaffa
VICTORIA
Great
Cape Howe
Cape Nelson
★ **Melbourne**
Cape Otway
Wilsons Promontory
N
W ✦ **E**
S
KING ISLAND
Bass Strait
FLINDERS ISLAND
TASMAN SEA
Cape Grim
Cape Portland
Mt. Ossa 5,305 Ft. △
Freycinet Peninsula
TASMANIA
★ **Hobart**
South East Cape
North Cape
Needles Point
Auckland
NORTH ISLAND
Bay of Plenty
East Cape
Cape Egmont
△ Mt. Ruapehu
Cape Farewell
The Twins 5,990 Ft. △
NEW ZEALAND
⊛ **Wellington**
Aoraki 12,316 Ft. △
SOUTH ISLAND
Southern Alps
● **Christchurch**
Banks Peninsula
Cape Providence
● Dunedin
Foveaux Strait
STEWART ISLAND
CHATHAM ISLANDS

0 100 200 300 400 500 Miles
0 200 400 600 800 Kilometers
Scale 1:20,000,000; one inch to 315 miles
Copyright by Rand McNally & Co.
Made in U.S.A.
N-CMW95000-A1- -1-1-1

Land Elevation Feet (Meters)

9,840 and over (3,000 and over)
6,560 - 9,840 (2,000 - 3,000)
3,280 - 6,560 (1,000 - 2,000)
1,640 - 3,280 (500 - 1,000)
656 - 1,640 (200 - 500)
0 - 656 feet (0 - 200)

THE LAND

Desert wastelands of sand and rock blanket the central and western parts of Australia, while a broad band of dry grasslands surrounds the deserts. Only about six percent of Australia's land is suitable for farming. Most Australians live along the southeastern coast, between the ocean and the long chain of mountains and plateaus known as the Great Dividing Range. Manufacturing and service industries flourish in this region. New Zealand, Australia's neighbor to the southeast, includes mountains, fjords, glaciers, rain forests, and geysers. Thanks to its small population and lack of heavy industry, it is one of the least polluted countries in the world. New Guinea, which lies to the north of Australia, is the second-largest island in the world. High, jagged mountains form a long spine across its width, wide swampy plains line its coasts, and tropical rain forests cover much of the island. Most of the other islands of Oceania were formed by volcanoes.

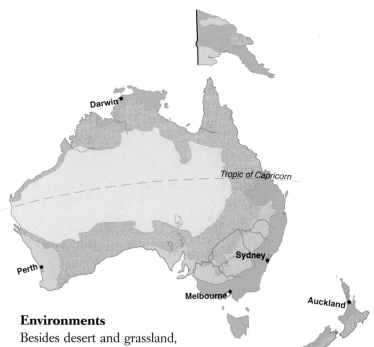

Environments
Besides desert and grassland, Australia also has forests, swamps, and mountains. Mountains cover two-thirds of New Zealand. New Guinea's dense rain forests, with their valuable hardwood trees, are an important natural resource, as are the palm trees that grow on many of the other islands of Oceania.

Environments
- Forest
- Swamp
- Crop and woodland
- Cropland
- Crop and grazing land
- Grassland
- Desert
- Tundra
- Barren
- Urban

Mineral processing facilities can be found throughout Australia.

Manufacturing
Manufacturing plays a central role in Australia's economy, with the refinement of metals and other natural resources topping the list of industries. The country also produces chemicals, plastics, textiles, and other durable goods. Traditionally, New Zealand has produced few manufactured goods, but its food-processing and paper manufacturing industries have been expanding. Most of the other countries in Oceania do not produce manufactured goods.

Much of Australia's interior, called the Outback, consists of semiarid plains that harbor hearty plants and animals.

Wool
With more than 14 percent of the world's sheep, Australia produces more wool than any other country on Earth. The largest sheep "stations," or ranches, cover more than 5,000 square miles (12,900 square kilometers). New Zealand ranks as the second-largest wool producer; nearly half of its land is used as pasture.

Sheep outnumber people in Australia by a ratio of seven to one. In New Zealand, the ratio is 14 to 1.

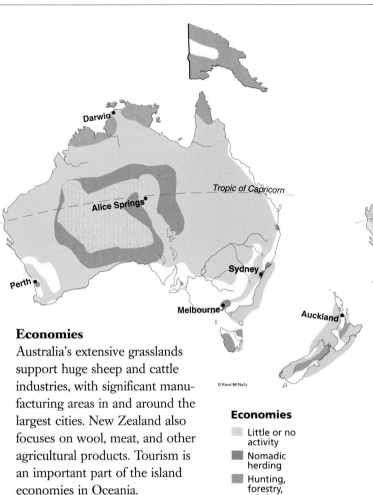

Economies

Australia's extensive grasslands support huge sheep and cattle industries, with significant manufacturing areas in and around the largest cities. New Zealand also focuses on wool, meat, and other agricultural products. Tourism is an important part of the island economies in Oceania.

Economies

- Little or no activity
- Nomadic herding
- Hunting, forestry, subsistence farming
- Forestry
- Agriculture
- Stock raising
- Manufacturing, commerce
- Fishing

Miners sift through mounds of sediment to uncover opals, iridescent gemstones that are exported.

Gems and Minerals

White, black, and fire opals mined in southern Australia are world-famous, but Australia is also an important source of diamonds: Its mines produce thirty percent of the world's supply. Australia's many other mineral resources include iron ore, coal, uranium, lead, zinc, copper, nickel, and natural gas. New Zealand has large reserves of coal, natural gas, and oil, while New Guinea's greatest sources of mineral wealth are copper, gold, and silver.

Not all diamonds become jewelry; industries use them to cut hard surfaces.

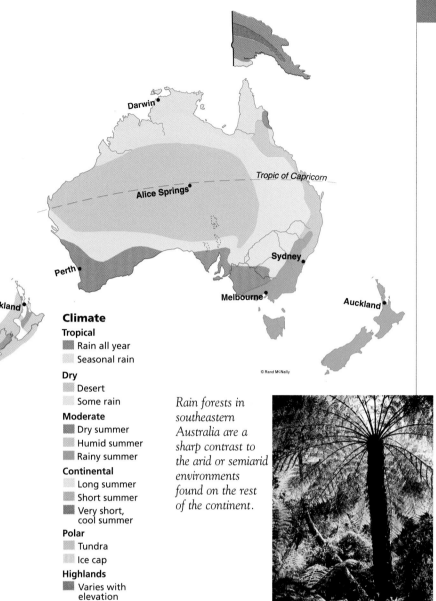

Climate

Tropical
- Rain all year
- Seasonal rain

Dry
- Desert
- Some rain

Moderate
- Dry summer
- Humid summer
- Rainy summer

Continental
- Long summer
- Short summer
- Very short, cool summer

Polar
- Tundra
- Ice cap

Highlands
- Varies with elevation

Rain forests in southeastern Australia are a sharp contrast to the arid or semiarid environments found on the rest of the continent.

Climate

In central and western Australia, the climate is very hot and dry. Near the coasts, especially in the southeast and the north, rain is more abundant and temperatures are cooler. New Zealand's climate is generally milder and wetter than Australia's. New Guinea and most other parts of Oceania have hot tropical climates.

Tourism

Tourists are drawn to Australia's natural wonders as well as to the fun-loving, easygoing lifestyle of Australians. Scenic New Zealand also enjoys a booming tourist industry. The tropical islands of Oceania have long been popular vacation spots, especially for sun-seeking Europeans and Americans.

Airplanes provide a spectacular view of the Great Barrier Reef.

THE PEOPLE

Although Australia is one of the largest countries in the world, it has a relatively small population. Very few people live in its vast interior–the Outback. Most Australians live near the coast, especially along the southeastern stretch that includes Sydney, Melbourne, Brisbane, and Adelaide. Although the Aborigines were the earliest humans to settle the continent, they make up only one percent of Australia's population today. Most Australians are descendants of British settlers, but in recent years immigrants from all over the world have added diversity to the continent's ethnic makeup. New Zealand's population is similar to Australia's, but its native people, the Maoris, represent ten percent of the population. Due to centuries of isolation, the island groups of Oceania have retained their distinct cultures. There has been little immigration there from other parts of the world.

The Aborigine culture includes many ceremonial dances and rituals.

A father and son ride around their farm in Australia.

Boating is a popular pasttime for tourists in Australia and New Zealand.

Australia's large population of kangaroos often comes into contact with humans.

10   11   12   13   14   15   16   17

The Aborigines developed boomerangs to aid them in hunting animals.

Australia & Oceania Facts

Population: 29,900,000

Population Density: 9.1 people per square mile (3.5 per square kilometer)

Most Populous Country: Australia, 18,735,000 people

Largest City: Sydney, Australia, 3,740,000 people (metropolitan area)

N
W   E
S

These schoolgirls in Sydney exhibit Australia's easygoing manner.

Torres Strait
Cape York
Bamaga
Weipa
Duifken Point
Cape York Peninsula

Gulf of Carpentaria

CORAL SEA

Cooktown

Normanton
...ketown
Cairns
Halifax Bay
Camooweal
Townsville
Cloncurry
Hughenden
Mackay
...ount Isa
Winton
Blair Athol
Great Artesian Basin
Longreach
Emerald
Cape Capricorn
Rockhampton
Barcaldine
Springsure
Gladstone
Yaraka
Blackall
Tropic of Capricorn
Theodore
Bundaberg
QUEENSLAND
Maryborough
Sandy Cape
Charleville
Mitchell
FRASER ISLAND
Chinchilla
Gympie
Toowoomba
Redcliffe
Innamincka
Thargomindah
Cunnamulla
Ipswich
★ **Brisbane**
Warwick
Southport
Cape Byron
Lake Eyre North
Lismore
Marree
Milparinka
Bourke
Grafton
Lake Torrens
Armidale
Coffs Harbour
Tamworth
Wilcannia
Nyngan
Taree
Port Augusta
Broken Hill
Dubbo
Whyalla
NEW SOUTH WALES
Cessnock
Newcastle
Port Pirie
Penrith
★ **Sydney**
Elizabeth
Mildura
Griffith
Campbelltown
Adelaide
Goulburn
Wollongong
Wagga Wagga
A.C.T.
Jervis Bay
VICTORIA
Albury
Canberra
Encounter Bay
Wangaratta
Bendigo
Cooma
Cape Jaffa
Horsham
Ballarat
Mt. Kosciuszko 7,313 Ft.
Cape Howe
Hamilton
Geelong
★ **Melbourne**
Mount Gambier
Portland
Moe
Sale
Cape Otway
Wilsons Promontory

Murray
Darling
Barwon
Copper Creek

PACIFIC OCEAN

TASMAN SEA

KING ISLAND
Bass Strait
FLINDERS ISLAND
Cape Grim
Burnie
Devonport
Zeehan
Launceston
TASMANIA
Hobart
South East Cape

NORFOLK ISLAND (Austl.)

North Cape
NORTH ISLAND
Whangarei
East Coast Bays
Manukau ● **Auckland**
Hamilton
Bay of Plenty
Tauranga
New Plymouth
Cape Egmont
Taupo
Rotorua
East Cape
Gisborne
Wanganui
Napier
Cape Farewell
Hastings
Nelson
Palmerston North
Greymouth
Porirua
Aoraki 12,316 Ft.
Haast
Cook Strait
Wellington
SOUTH ISLAND
Waiau
NEW ZEALAND
Cape Providence
Manapouri
Ashburton
Christchurch
Oamaru
Southern Alps
Invercargill
Foveaux Strait
Dunedin
STEWART ISLAND

CHATHAM ISLANDS (N.Z.)

0   100   200   300   400   500 Miles
0   200   400   600   800 Kilometers

Scale 1:20,000,000; one inch to 315 miles
Copyright by Rand McNally & Co.
Made in U.S.A.
N-CMW95000-P1- -:-:-1

PACIFIC ISLANDS

Scattered across a vast area in the Pacific Ocean, the islands of Oceania feature landscapes as varied as the alpine terrain of New Zealand's South Island, the mountain rain forests of Papua New Guinea, and the flower- and palm-strewn atolls of Polynesia. Papua New Guinea, which occupies the western portion of the island of New Guinea, is Oceania's largest country. It is a land of broad ethnic variety: More than 700 dialects are spoken there, although English is the official language. To the east of Papua New Guinea lies the group of islands known as Melanesia, a name that means "black islands." To the north and east of Melanesia is Micronesia, which means "small islands," and farther east lies Polynesia, or "many islands." These far-flung volcanic islands and coral atolls were originally settled by seafaring peoples from the Asian mainland who brought their plants, animals, and cultures with them as they ventured as far as Hawaii and Easter Island in huge canoes.

Snowcapped Aoraki, or Mount Cook, is New Zealand's highest mountain.

The starfish plays an important role in Oceania's reef systems.

10   11   12   13   14   15   16   17"

New Zealand, called "Aotearoa" or "long white cloud" by its original Maori inhabitants, is the second-largest country in Oceania (after Australia). Most people live on North Island in Auckland and Wellington. While South Island is known for its mountains and deep fjords, North Island has its share of wonders: Glowworms light deep cave chambers, while hot springs and geysers provide geothermal power and heat for the island's inhabitants. New Zealand has far more sheep than people, and wool and mutton are two of its leading exports.

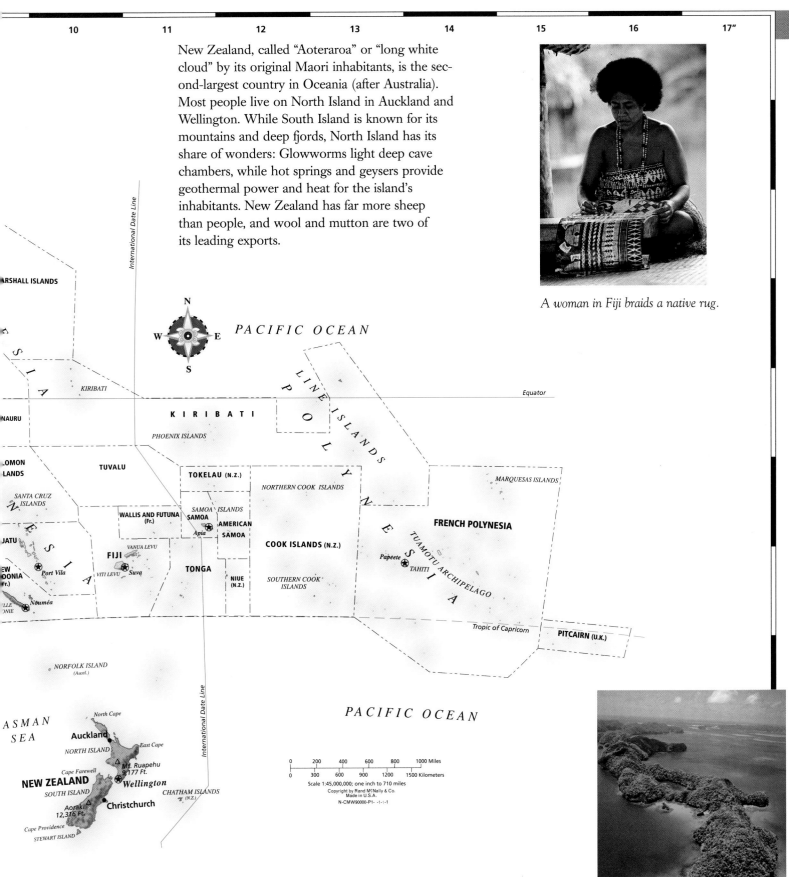

A woman in Fiji braids a native rug.

PACIFIC OCEAN

Equator

MARSHALL ISLANDS

KIRIBATI

KIRIBATI

NAURU

PHOENIX ISLANDS

LINE ISLANDS

POLYNESIA

TUVALU

TOKELAU (N.Z.)

NORTHERN COOK ISLANDS

MARQUESAS ISLANDS

SOLOMON ISLANDS

SANTA CRUZ ISLANDS

WALLIS AND FUTUNA (Fr.)

SAMOA ISLANDS

SAMOA

Apia

AMERICAN SAMOA

FRENCH POLYNESIA

VANUA LEVU

FIJI

VITI LEVU   Suva

COOK ISLANDS (N.Z.)

TUAMOTU ARCHIPELAGO

VANUATU

Port Vila

TONGA

NIUE (N.Z.)

Papeete   TAHITI

NEW CALEDONIA (Fr.)

Nouméa

SOUTHERN COOK ISLANDS

Tropic of Capricorn

PITCAIRN (U.K.)

NORFOLK ISLAND (Austl.)

PACIFIC OCEAN

TASMAN SEA

North Cape

Auckland

East Cape

NORTH ISLAND

Cape Farewell

Mt. Ruapehu 9,177 Ft.

NEW ZEALAND

Wellington

SOUTH ISLAND

CHATHAM ISLANDS (N.Z.)

Aoraki 12,316 Ft.

Christchurch

Cape Providence

STEWART ISLAND

International Date Line

0 200 400 600 800 1000 Miles
0 300 600 900 1200 1500 Kilometers
Scale 1:45,000,000; one inch to 710 miles
Copyright by Rand McNally & Co.
Made in U.S.A.
N-CMW90000-P1- -1-1-1

Reefs dominate the volcanic island of Palau.

ANTARCTICA

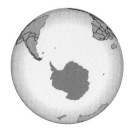

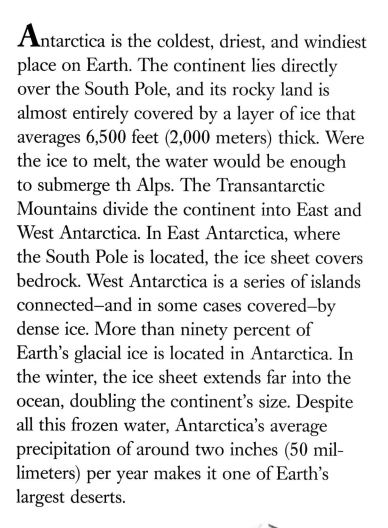

Antarctica is the coldest, driest, and windiest place on Earth. The continent lies directly over the South Pole, and its rocky land is almost entirely covered by a layer of ice that averages 6,500 feet (2,000 meters) thick. Were the ice to melt, the water would be enough to submerge th Alps. The Transantarctic Mountains divide the continent into East and West Antarctica. In East Antarctica, where the South Pole is located, the ice sheet covers bedrock. West Antarctica is a series of islands connected–and in some cases covered–by dense ice. More than ninety percent of Earth's glacial ice is located in Antarctica. In the winter, the ice sheet extends far into the ocean, doubling the continent's size. Despite all this frozen water, Antarctica's average precipitation of around two inches (50 millimeters) per year makes it one of Earth's largest deserts.

Antarctica Facts

Area: 5,400,000 square miles (14,000,000 square kilometers)

Highest Mountain: Vinson Massif, 16,066 feet (4,897 meters)

Lowest Point: Deep Lake, -184 feet (-56 meters)

Coldest Spot: Vostok, July 21, 1983, -129° Fahrenheit (-89° Celsius)

Very little plant life can survive in such cold conditions, but certain lichens, molds, mosses, fungi, algae, and bacteria live in this arctic habitat.

Antarctica has no permanent residents. Instead, groups of researchers from all over the world come to visit scientific stations and to learn more about this forbidding, fascinating continent.

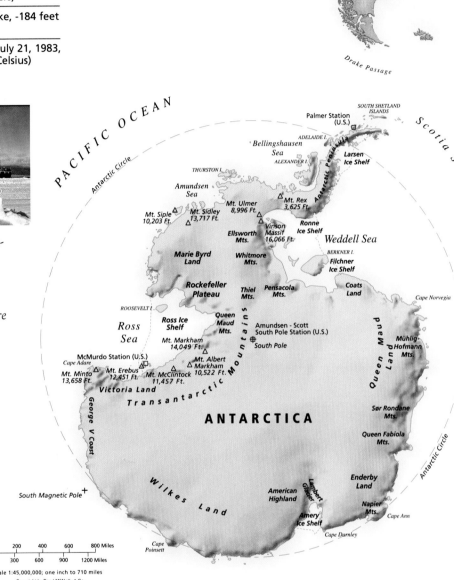

Drake Passage

PACIFIC OCEAN

Antarctic Circle

SOUTH SHETLAND ISLANDS

Palmer Station (U.S.)

ADELAIDE I.

Bellingshausen Sea

ALEXANDER I.

Larsen Ice Shelf

Antarctic Peninsula

Scotia Sea

THURSTON I.

Mt. Rex 3,625 Ft.

Amundsen Sea

Mt. Ulmer 8,996 Ft.

Mt. Siple 10,203 Ft.

Mt. Sidley 13,717 Ft.

Vinson Massif 16,066 Ft.

Ronne Ice Shelf

Ellsworth Mts.

Weddell Sea

Marie Byrd Land

Whitmore Mts.

BERKNER I.

Filchner Ice Shelf

Rockefeller Plateau

Thiel Mts.

Pensacola Mts.

Coats Land

Cape Norvegia

ATLANTIC OCEAN

ROOSEVELT I.

Ross Sea

Ross Ice Shelf

Queen Maud Mts.

Amundsen - Scott South Pole Station (U.S.)

South Pole

Queen Maud Land

Mühlig-Hofmann Mts.

Mt. Markham 14,049 Ft.

McMurdo Station (U.S.)

Cape Adare

Mt. Minto 13,658 Ft.

Mt. Erebus 12,451 Ft.

Mt. McClintock 11,457 Ft.

Mt. Albert Markham 10,522 Ft.

Transantarctic Mountains

Sør Rondane Mts.

Victoria Land

ANTARCTICA

Queen Fabiola Mts.

George V Coast

South Magnetic Pole +

Wilkes Land

American Highland

Lambert Glacier

Enderby Land

Napier Mts.

Antarctic Circle

Cape Ann

Amery Ice Shelf

Cape Darnley

Cape Poinsett

```
0    200   400   600   800 Miles
0    300   600   900   1200 Miles
```
Scale 1:45,000,000; one inch to 710 miles
Copyright by Rand McNally & Co.
Made in U.S.A.
N-CMW94000-P1- -1-1-1

INDIAN OCEAN

Seabirds flock to Antarctica to roost, and several different species of penguin (above left) live on the ice, near the coast (left). No land mammals live here, but an abundance of krill—tiny shrimplike creatures—provides food for a large population of aquatic mammals, including a variety of whales (below) and seals.

Country Flag and Fact File

North America

Anguilla (U.K.)
Area: 35 sq mi (91 sq km)
Population: 11,000
Capital: The Valley

Antigua and Barbuda
Area: 171 sq mi (442 sq km)
Population: 64,000
Capital: St. John's

Bahamas
Area: 5,382 sq mi
  (13,939 sq km)
Population: 282,000
Capital: Nassau

Barbados
Area: 166 sq mi (430 sq km)
Population: 259,000
Capital: Bridgetown

Belize
Area: 8,866 sq mi
  (22,963 sq km)
Population: 233,000
Capital: Belmopan

Canada
Area: 3,849,674 sq mi
  (9,970,610 sq km)
Population: 30,450,000
Capital: Ottawa

Costa Rica
Area: 19,730 sq mi
  (51,100 sq km)
Population: 3,639,000
Capital: San José

Cuba
Area: 42,804 sq mi
  (110,861 sq km)
Population: 11,075,000
Capital: Havana

Dominica
Area: 305 sq mi (790 sq km)
Population: 66,000
Capital: Roseau

Dominican Republic
Area: 18,704 sq mi
  (48,442 sq km)
Population: 8,064,000
Capital: Santo Domingo

El Salvador
Area: 8,124 sq mi
  (21,041 sq km)
Population: 5,797,000
Capital: San Salvador

Greenland (Denmark)
Area: 840,004 sq mi
  (2,175,600 sq km)
Population: 59,000
Capital: Godthåb

Grenada
Area: 133 sq mi (344 sq km)
Population: 96,000
Capital: St. George's

Guatemala
Area: 42,042 sq mi
  (108,889 sq km)
Population: 12,170,000
Capital: Guatemala

Haiti
Area: 10,714 sq mi
  (27,750 sq km)
Population: 6,833,000
Capital: Port-au-Prince

Honduras
Area: 43,277 sq mi
  (112,088 sq km)
Population: 5,931,000
Capital: Tegucigalpa

Jamaica
Area: 4,244 sq mi
  (10,991 sq km)
Population: 2,644,000
Capital: Kingston

Mexico
Area: 759,533 sq mi
  (1,967,183 sq km)
Population: 99,430,000
Capital: Mexico City

Nicaragua
Area: 50,054 sq mi
  (129,640 sq km)
Population: 4,650,000
Capital: Managua

Panama
Area: 29,157 sq mi
  (75,517 sq km)
Population: 2,757,000
Capital: Panamá

Puerto Rico (U.S.)
Area: 3,515 sq mi
  (9,104 sq km)
Population: 3,870,000
Capital: San Juan

St. Kitts and Nevis
Area: 104 sq mi (269 sq km)
Population: 42,000
Capital: Basseterre

St. Lucia
Area: 238 sq mi (616 sq km)
Population: 153,000
Capital: Castries

**St. Vincent and the
Grenadines**
Area: 150 sq mi (388 sq km)
Population: 120,000
Capital: Kingstown

Trinidad and Tobago
Area: 1,980 sq mi
  (5,128 sq km)
Population: 1,110,000
Capital: Port of Spain

United States
Area: 3,787,425 sq mi
  (9,809,431 sq km)
Population: 271,490,000
Capital: Washington

South America

Argentina
Area: 1,073,519 sq mi
(2,780,400 sq km)
Population: 36,500,000
Capitals: Buenos Aires (de facto) and Viedma (future)

Bolivia
Area: 424,165 sq mi
(1,098,581 sq km)
Population: 7,904,000
Capitals: La Paz (seat of government) and Sucre (legal capital)

Brazil
Area: 3,300,172 sq mi
(8,547,404 sq km)
Population: 170,860,000
Capital: Brasília

Chile
Area: 292,135 sq mi
(756,626 sq km)
Population: 14,880,000
Capital: Santiago

Colombia
Area: 440,831 sq mi
(1,141,748 sq km)
Population: 38,950,000
Capital: Bogotá

Ecuador
Area: 105,037 sq mi
(272,045 sq km)
Population: 12,450,000
Capital: Quito

Guyana
Area: 83,000 sq mi
(214,969 sq km)
Population: 706,000
Capital: Georgetown

Paraguay
Area: 157,048 sq mi
(406,752 sq km)
Population: 5,362,000
Capital: Asunción

Peru
Area: 496,225 sq mi
(1,285,216 sq km)
Population: 26,365,000
Capital: Lima

Suriname
Area: 63,251 sq mi
(163,820 sq km)
Population: 430,000
Capital: Paramaribo

Uruguay
Area: 68,500 sq mi
(177,414 sq km)
Population: 3,297,000
Capital: Montevideo

Venezuela
Area: 352,144 sq mi
(912,050 sq km)
Population: 23,005,000
Capital: Caracas

Europe

Albania
Area: 11,100 sq mi
(28,748 sq km)
Population: 3,347,000
Capital: Tiranë

Andorra
Area: 175 sq mi
(453 sq km)
Population: 65,000
Capital: Andorra

Austria
Area: 32,377 sq mi
(83,856 sq km)
Population: 8,136,000
Capital: Vienna

Belarus
Area: 80,155 sq mi
(207,600 sq km)
Population: 10,405,000
Capital: Minsk

Belgium
Area: 11,783 sq mi
(30,518 sq km)
Population: 10,180,000
Capital: Brussels

Bosnia and Herzegovina
Area: 19,741 sq mi
(51,129 sq km)
Population: 3,427,000
Capital: Sarajevo

Bulgaria
Area: 42,855 sq mi
(110,994 sq km)
Population: 8,215,000
Capital: Sofia

Croatia
Area: 21,829 sq mi
(56,538 sq km)
Population: 4,675,000
Capital: Zagreb

Czech Republic
Area: 30,450 sq mi
(78,864 sq km)
Population: 10,280,000
Capital: Prague

Denmark
Area: 16,639 sq mi
(43,094 sq km)
Population: 5,347,000
Capital: Copenhagen

Estonia
Area: 17,413 sq mi
(45,100 sq km)
Population: 1,414,000
Capital: Tallinn

Finland
Area: 130,559 sq mi
(338,145 sq km)
Population: 5,154,000
Capital: Helsinki

France
Area: 211,208 sq mi
(547,026 sq km)
Population: 58,890,000
Capital: Paris

Germany
Area: 137,822 sq mi
(356,955 sq km)
Population: 82,700,000
Capital: Berlin

Greece
Area: 50,949 sq mi
  (131,957 sq km)
Population: 10,685,000
Capital: Athens

Hungary
Area: 35,919 sq mi
  (93,030 sq km)
Population: 10,195,000
Capital: Budapest

Iceland
Area: 39,769 sq mi
  (103,000 sq km)
Population: 272,000
Capital: Reykjavík

Ireland
Area: 27,137 sq mi
  (70,285 sq km)
Population: 3,626,000
Capital: Dublin

Italy
Area: 116,336 sq mi
  (301,309 sq km)
Population: 56,760,000
Capital: Rome

Latvia
Area: 24,595 sq mi
  (63,700 sq km)
Population: 2,368,000
Capital: Rīga

Liechtenstein
Area: 62 sq mi (160 sq km)
Population: 32,000
Capital: Vaduz

Lithuania
Area: 25,213 sq mi
  (65,300 sq km)
Population: 3,592,000
Capital: Vilnius

Luxembourg
Area: 999 sq mi
  (2,586 sq km)
Population: 427,000
Capital: Luxembourg

Macedonia
Area: 9,928 sq mi
  (25,713 sq km)
Population: 2,016,000
Capital: Skopje

Malta
Area: 122 sq mi (316 sq km)
Population: 381,000
Capital: Valletta

Moldova
Area: 13,012 sq mi
  (33,700 sq km)
Population: 4,459,000
Capital: Chişinău

Monaco
Area: 0.8 sq mi (2 sq km)
Population: 32,000
Capital: Monaco

Netherlands
Area: 16,164 sq mi
  (41,864 sq km)
Population: 15,770,000
Capitals: Amsterdam
  (designated) and The Hague
  (seat of government)

Norway
Area: 149,405 sq mi
  (386,958 sq km)
Population: 4,430,000
Capital: Oslo

Poland
Area: 121,196 sq mi
  (313,895 sq km)
Population: 38,600,000
Capital: Warsaw

Portugal
Area: 35,516 sq mi
  (91,985 sq km)
Population: 9,925,000
Capital: Lisbon

Romania
Area: 91,699 sq mi
  (237,500 sq km)
Population: 22,360,000
Capital: Bucharest

San Marino
Area: 24 sq mi (61 sq km)
Population: 25,000
Capital: San Marino

Slovakia
Area: 18,933 sq mi
  (49,035 sq km)
Population: 5,395,000
Capital: Bratislava

Slovenia
Area: 7,820 sq mi
  (20,253 sq km)
Population: 1,971,000
Capital: Ljubljana

Spain
Area: 194,885 sq mi
  (504,750 sq km)
Population: 39,150,000
Capital: Madrid

Sweden
Area: 173,732 sq mi
  (449,964 sq km)
Population: 8,899,000
Capital: Stockholm

Switzerland
Area: 15,943 sq mi
  (41,293 sq km)
Population: 7,268,000
Capital: Bern

Ukraine
Area: 233,090 sq mi
  (603,700 sq km)
Population: 49,965,000
Capital: Kiev

United Kingdom
Area: 94,249 sq mi
  (244,101 sq km)
Population: 59,040,000
Capital: London

Vatican City
Area: 0.2 sq mi (0.4 sq km)
Population: 1,000
Capital: Vatican City

Yugoslavia
Area: 39,449 sq mi
  (102,173 sq km)
Population: 11,205,000
Capital: Belgrade

Africa

Algeria
Area: 919,595 sq mi
(2,381,741 sq km)
Population: 30,805,000
Capital: Algiers

Angola
Area: 481,354 sq mi
(1,246,700 sq km)
Population: 11,020,000
Capital: Luanda

Benin
Area: 43,475 sq mi
(112,600 sq km)
Population: 6,202,000
Capitals: Porto-Novo
(designated) and Cotonou
(de facto)

Botswana
Area: 224,711 sq mi
(582,000 sq km)
Population: 1,456,000
Capital: Gaborone

Burkina Faso
Area: 105,869 sq mi
(274,200 sq km)
Population: 11,420,000
Capital: Ouagadougou

Burundi
Area: 10,745 sq mi
(27,830 sq km)
Population: 5,634,000
Capital: Bujumbura

Cameroon
Area: 183,568 sq mi
(475,440 sq km)
Population: 15,240,000
Capital: Yaoundé

Cape Verde
Area: 1,557 sq mi
(4,033 sq km)
Population: 403,000
Capital: Praia

Central African Republic
Area: 240,535 sq mi
(622,984 sq km)
Population: 3,410,000
Capital: Bangui

Chad
Area: 495,755 sq mi
(1,284,000 sq km)
Population: 7,458,000
Capital: N'Djamena

Comoros
Area: 863 sq mi
(2,235 sq km)
Population: 554,000
Capital: Moroni

Congo
Area: 132,047 sq mi
(342,000 sq km)
Population: 2,688,000
Capital: Brazzaville

Cote d'Ivoire
Area: 124,518 sq mi
(322,500 sq km)
Population: 15,630,000
Capitals: Abidjan (de facto)
and Yamoussoukro (future)

Dem. Rep. of the Congo
Area: 905,446 sq mi
(2,345,095 sq km)
Population: 49,735,000
Capital: Kinshasa

Djibouti
Area: 8,958 sq mi
(23,200 sq km)
Population: 444,000
Capital: Djibouti

Egypt
Area: 386,662 sq mi
(1,001,449 sq km)
Population: 66,660,000
Capital: Cairo

Equatorial Guinea
Area: 10,831 sq mi
(28,051 sq km)
Population: 460,000
Capital: Malabo

Eritrea
Area: 36,170 sq mi
(93,679 sq km)
Population: 3,907,000
Capital: Asmera

Ethiopia
Area: 446,953 sq mi
(1,157,603 sq km)
Population: 59,040,000
Capital: Addis Ababa

Gabon
Area: 103,347 sq mi
(267,667 sq km)
Population: 1,217,000
Capital: Libreville

The Gambia
Area: 4,127 sq mi
(10,689 sq km)
Population: 1,314,000
Capital: Banjul

Ghana
Area: 92,098 sq mi
(238,533 sq km)
Population: 18,695,000
Capital: Accra

Guinea
Area: 94,926 sq mi
(245,857 sq km)
Population: 7,508,000
Capital: Conakry

Guinea-Bissau
Area: 13,948 sq mi
(36,125 sq km)
Population: 1,220,000
Capital: Bissau

Kenya
Area: 224,961 sq mi
(582,646 sq km)
Population: 28,580,000
Capital: Nairobi

Lesotho
Area: 11,720 sq mi
(30,355 sq km)
Population: 2,110,000
Capital: Maseru

Liberia
Area: 38,250 sq mi
(99,067 sq km)
Population: 2,852,000
Capital: Monrovia

Libya
Area: 679,362 sq mi
  (1,759,540 sq km)
Population: 4,934,000
Capital: Tripoli

Madagascar
Area: 226,658 sq mi
  (587,041 sq km)
Population: 14,665,000
Capital: Antananarivo

Malawi
Area: 45,747 sq mi
  (118,484 sq km)
Population: 9,922,000
Capital: Lilongwe

Mali
Area: 482,077 sq mi
  (1,248,574 sq km)
Population: 10,275,000
Capital: Bamako

Mauritania
Area: 397,955 sq mi
  (1,030,700 sq km)
Population: 2,543,000
Capital: Nouakchott

Mauritius
Area: 788 sq mi (2,040 sq km)
Population: 1,175,000
Capital: Port Louis

Morocco
Area: 172,414 sq mi
  (446,550 sq km)
Population: 29,390,000
Capital: Rabat

Mozambique
Area: 308,642 sq mi
  (799,380 sq km)
Population: 19,895,000
Capital: Maputo

Namibia
Area: 317,818 sq mi
  (823,144 sq km)
Population: 1,635,000
Capital: Windhoek

Niger
Area: 489,191 sq mi
  (1,267,000 sq km)
Population: 9,815,000
Capital: Niamey

Nigeria
Area: 356,669 sq mi
  (923,768 sq km)
Population: 112,170,000
Capital: Abuja

Rwanda
Area: 10,169 sq mi
  (26,338 sq km)
Population: 8,055,000
Capital: Kigali

Sao Tome and Principe
Area: 372 sq mi (964 sq km)
Population: 152,000
Capital: São Tomé

Senegal
Area: 75,951 sq mi
  (196,712 sq km)
Population: 9,885,000
Capital: Dakar

Seychelles
Area: 175 sq mi (453 sq km)
Population: 79,000
Capital: Victoria

Sierra Leone
Area: 27,925 sq mi
  (72,325 sq km)
Population: 5,182,000
Capital: Freetown

Somalia
Area: 246,201 sq mi
  (637,657 sq km)
Population: 6,993,000
Capital: Mogadishu

South Africa
Area: 471,009 sq mi
  (1,219,909 sq km)
Population: 43,140,000
Capitals: Pretoria
  (administrative), Cape
  Town (legislative), and
  Bloemfontein (judicial)

Sudan
Area: 967,499 sq mi
  (2,505,813 sq km)
Population: 34,010,000
Capital: Khartoum

Swaziland
Area: 6,704 sq mi
  (17,364 sq km)
Population: 975,000
Capitals: Mbabane
  (administrative) and
  Lobamba (legislative)

Tanzania
Area: 364,900 sq mi
  (945,087 sq km)
Population: 30,935,000
Capitals: Dar es Salaam
  (de facto) and Dodoma
  (legislative)

Togo
Area: 21,925 sq mi
  (56,785 sq km)
Population: 4,992,000
Capital: Lomé

Tunisia
Area: 63,170 sq mi
  (163,610 sq km)
Population: 9,448,000
Capital: Tunis

Uganda
Area: 93,104 sq mi
  (241,139 sq km)
Population: 22,485,000
Capital: Kampala

Zambia
Area: 290,586 sq mi
  (752,614 sq km)
Population: 9,561,000
Capital: Lusaka

Zimbabwe
Area: 150,873 sq mi
  (390,759 sq km)
Population: 11,105,000
Capital: Harare

Asia

Afghanistan
Area: 251,826 sq mi
 (652,225 sq km)
Population: 25,315,000
Capital: Kabul

Armenia
Area: 11,506 sq mi
 (29,800 sq km)
Population: 3,416,000
Capital: Yerevan

Azerbaijan
Area: 33,436 sq mi
 (86,600 sq km)
Population: 7,883,000
Capital: Baku

Bahrain
Area: 267 sq mi (691 sq km)
Population: 622,000
Capital: Al Manāmah

Bangladesh
Area: 55,598 sq mi
 (143,998 sq km)
Population: 126,110,000
Capital: Dhaka

Bhutan
Area: 17,954 sq mi
 (46,500 sq km)
Population: 1,930,000
Capital: Thimphu

Brunei
Area: 2,226 sq mi
 (5,765 sq km)
Population: 319,000
Capital: Bandar Seri Begawan

Cambodia
Area: 69,898 sq mi
 (181,035 sq km)
Population: 11,485,000
Capital: Phnum Pénh

China
Area: 3,690,045 sq mi
 (9,557,172 sq km)
Population: 1,242,070,000
Capital: Beijing

Cyprus
Area: 2,277 sq mi
 (5,896 sq km)
Population: 615,000
Capital: Nicosia

Georgia
Area: 26,911 sq mi
 (69,700 sq km)
Population: 5,085,000
Capital: Tbilisi

India
Area: 1,237,061 sq mi
 (3,203,975 sq km)
Population: 992,470,000
Capital: New Delhi

Indonesia
Area: 752,409 sq mi
 (1,948,732 sq km)
Population: 214,530,000
Capital: Jakarta

Iran
Area: 630,578 sq mi
 (1,633,189 sq km)
Population: 64,830,000
Capital: Tehrān

Iraq
Area: 169,235 sq mi
 (438,317 sq km)
Population: 22,070,000
Capital: Baghdād

Israel
Area: 8,019 sq mi
 (20,770 sq km)
Population: 5,353,000
Capital: Jerusalem

Japan
Area: 145,850 sq mi
 (377,750 sq km)
Population: 126,060,000
Capital: Tōkyō

Jordan
Area: 35,135 sq mi
 (91,000 sq km)
Population: 4,491,000
Capital: 'Ammān

Kazakhstan
Area: 1,049,155 sq mi
 (2,717,300 sq km)
Population: 16,835,000
Capital: Astana

Kuwait
Area: 6,880 sq mi
 (17,818 sq km)
Population: 1,952,000
Capital: Kuwait

Kyrgyzstan
Area: 76,641 sq mi
 (198,500 sq km)
Population: 4,531,000
Capital: Bishkek

Laos
Area: 91,429 sq mi
 (236,800 sq km)
Population: 5,334,000
Capital: Viangchan

Lebanon
Area: 4,016 sq mi
 (10,400 sq km)
Population: 3,534,000
Capital: Beirut

Malaysia
Area: 127,320 sq mi
 (329,758 sq km)
Population: 21,155,000
Capital: Kuala Lumpur

Maldives
Area: 115 sq mi (298 sq km)
Population: 295,000
Capital: Male'

Mongolia
Area: 604,829 sq mi
 (1,566,500 sq km)
Population: 2,599,000
Capital: Ulan Bator

Myanmar
Area: 261,228 sq mi
 (676,578 sq km)
Population: 47,700,000
Capital: Yangon

Nepal
Area: 56,827 sq mi
  (147,181 sq km)
Population: 23,995,000
Capital: Kathmandu

North Cyprus
Area: 1,295 sq mi
  (3,355 sq km)
Population: 137,000
Capital: Nicosia

North Korea
Area: 46,540 sq mi
(120,538 sq km)
Population: 21,230,000
Capital: P'yŏngyang

Oman
Area: 82,030 sq mi
  (212,457 sq km)
Population: 2,405,000
Capital: Muscat

Pakistan
Area: 339,732 sq mi
  (879,902 sq km)
Population: 136,620,000
Capital: Islāmābād

Philippines
Area: 115,831 sq mi
  (300,000 sq km)
Population: 78,530,000
Capital: Manila

Qatar
Area: 4,412 sq mi
  (11,427 sq km)
Population: 710,000
Capital: Doha

Russia
Area: 6,592,849 sq mi
  (17,075,400 sq km)
Population: 146,630,000
Capital: Moscow

Saudi Arabia
Area: 830,000 sq mi
  (2,149,690 sq km)
Population: 21,140,000
Capital: Riyadh

Singapore
Area: 246 sq mi (636 sq km)
Population: 3,511,000
Capital: Singapore

South Korea
Area: 38,230 sq mi
  (99,016 sq km)
Population: 46,650,000
Capital: Seoul

Sri Lanka
Area: 24,962 sq mi
  (64,652 sq km)
Population: 19,040,000
Capitals: Colombo
  (designated) and
  Sri Jayawardenepura
  (seat of government)

Syria
Area: 71,498 sq mi
  (185,180 sq km)
Population: 16,955,000
Capital: Damascus

Taiwan
Area: 13,900 sq mi
  (36,002 sq km)
Population: 22,010,000
Capital: T'aipei

Tajikistan
Area: 55,251 sq mi
  (143,100 sq km)
Population: 6,059,000
Capital: Dushanbe

Thailand
Area: 198,115 sq mi
  (513,115 sq km)
Population: 60,330,000
Capital: Bangkok

Turkey
Area: 300,948 sq mi
  (779,452 sq km)
Population: 65,090,000
Capital: Ankara

Turkmenistan
Area: 188,456 sq mi
  (488,100 sq km)
Population: 4,332,000
Capital: Ashgabat

United Arab Emirates
Area: 32,278 sq mi
  (83,600 sq km)
Population: 2,323,000
Capital: Abu Dhabi

Uzbekistan
Area: 172,742 sq mi
  (447,400 sq km)
Population: 23,940,000
Capital: Tashkent

Vietnam
Area: 127,428 sq mi
  (330,036 sq km)
Population: 76,790,000
Capital: Hanoi

Yemen
Area: 203,850 sq mi
  (527,968 sq km)
Population: 16,660,000
Capital: Sanaa

Australia and Oceania

Australia
Area: 2,966,155 sq mi
  (7,682,300 sq km)
Population: 18,735,000
Capital: Canberra

Cook Islands (New Zealand)
Area: 91 sq mi (236 sq km)
Population: 20,000
Capital: Avarua

Fiji
Area: 7,056 sq mi
  (18,274 sq km)
Population: 808,000
Capital: Suva

Kiribati
Area: 313 sq mi (811 sq km)
Population: 85,000
Capital: Bairiki

Marshall Islands
Area: 70 sq mi (181 sq km)
Population: 64,000
Capital: Majuro (island)

Federated States of Micronesia
Area: 271 sq mi (702 sq km)
Population: 132,000
Capital: Palikir

Nauru
Area: 8.1 sq mi (21 sq km)
Population: 11,000
Capital: Yaren District

New Zealand
Area: 104,454 sq mi
 (270,534 sq km)
Population: 3,644,000
Capital: Wellington

Niue (New Zealand)
Area: 100 sq mi (259 sq km)
Population: 1,600
Capital: Alofi

Northern Mariana Islands (U.S.)
Area: 184 sq mi (477 sq km)
Population: 68,000
Capital: Saipan (island)

Palau
Area: 196 sq mi (508 sq km)
Population: 18,000
Capitals: Koror (de facto)
 and Melekeok (future)

Papua New Guinea
Area: 178,703 sq mi
 (462,840 sq km)
Population: 4,652,000
Capital: Port Moresby

Samoa
Area: 1,093 sq mi
 (2,831 sq km)
Population: 228,000
Capital: Apia

Solomon Islands
Area: 10,954 sq mi
 (28,370 sq km)
Population: 448,000
Capital: Honaira

Tonga
Area: 288 sq mi
 (747 sq km)
Population: 108,000
Capital: Nuku'alofa

Tuvalu
Area: 10 sq mi (26 sq km)
Population: 10,000
Capital: Funafuti

Vanuatu
Area: 4,707 sq mi
 (12,190 sq km)
Population: 187,000
Capital: Port Vila

Territories and Dependencies

North America

Country Name	Area	Population	Capital
Aruba (Netherlands)	75 sq mi (193 sq km)	68,000	Oranjestad
Bermuda (U.K.)	21 sq mi (54 sq km)	62,000	Hamilton
British Virgin Islands (U.K.)	59 sq mi (153 sq km)	19,000	Road Town
Cayman Islands (U.K.)	100 sq mi (259 sq km)	39,000	George Town
Guadeloupe (France)	657 sq mi (1,702 sq km)	418,000	Basse-Terre
Martinique (France)	436 sq mi (1,128 sq km)	409,000	Fort-de-France
Montserrat (U.K.)	39 sq mi (102 sq km)	13,000	Plymouth
Netherlands Antilles (Netherlands)	309 sq mi (800 sq km)	207,000	Willemstad
St. Pierre and Miquelon (France)	93 sq mi (242 sq km)	7,000	Saint-Pierre
Turks and Caicos Islands (U.K.)	193 sq mi (500 sq km)	16,000	Grand Turk
Virgin Islands (U.S.)	133 sq mi (344 sq km)	119,000	Charlotte Amalie

South America

Falkland Islands (U.K.)	4,700 sq mi (12,173 sq km)	2,900	Stanley
French Guiana (France)	32,253 sq mi (83,534 sq km)	166,000	Cayenne
South Georgia and the South Sandwich Islands (U.K.)	1,450 sq mi (3,755 sq km)	none	none

Europe

Faroe Islands (Denmark)	540 sq mi (1,399 sq km)	42,000	Tórshavn
Gibraltar (U.K.)	2.3 sq mi (6.0 sq km)	29,000	Gibraltar
Guernsey (U.K.)	30 sq mi (78 sq km)	65,000	St. Peter Port
Isle of Man (U.K.)	221 sq mi (572 sq km)	75,000	Douglas
Jersey (U.K.)	45 sq mi (116 sq km)	89,000	St. Helier

Africa

British Indian Ocean Territory (U.K.)	23 sq mi (60 sq km)	none	none
Mayotte (France)	144 sq mi (374 sq km)	146,000	Mamoudzou
Reunion (France)	967 sq mi (2,504 sq km)	711,000	Saint-Denis
St. Helena (U.K.)	121 sq mi (314 sq km)	7,000	Jamestown
Spanish North Africa (Spain)	12 sq mi (32 sq km)	153,000	none

Australia and Oceania

American Samoa (U.S.)	77 sq mi (199 sq km)	63,000	Pago Pago
Christmas Island (Australia)	52 sq mi (135 sq km)	2,300	Settlement
Cocos Islands (Australia)	5.4 sq mi (14 sq km)	600	West Island
French Polynesia (France)	1,360 sq mi (3,521 sq km)	228,000	Papeete
Guam (U.S.)	209 sq mi (541 sq km)	150,000	Agana
Johnson Atoll (U.S.)	0.5 sq mi (1.3 sq km)	1,100	none
Midway Islands (U.S.)	2 sq mi (5.2 sq km)	140	none
New Caledonia (France)	7,172 sq mi (18,575 sq km)	196,000	Nouméa
Norfolk Island (France)	14 sq mi (36 sq km)	2,200	Kingston
Pitcairn (U.K.)	19 sq mi (49 sq km)	400	Adamstown
Tokelau (New Zealand)	4.6 sq mi (12 sq km)	1,400	none
Wake Island (U.S.)	3 sq mi (7.8 sq km)	200	none
Wallis and Futuna (France)	99 sq mi (255 sq km)	15,000	Mata-Utu

Glossary

A

agriculture Land use for the growing of crops and the raising of livestock; farming.

arid Extremely dry; lacking moisture.

B

border The region or line around the edge of a country, state, province, or territory that separates it from another country, state, province, or territory.

C

cape An expanse of land, shaped like a point, extending into water.

capital A city that is the seat of a country or state government.

cartographer A person who makes maps.

cash crop Crops grown to sell commercially, often to foreign countries.

climate Weather patterns within a region that happen over long periods of time.

continent A major landmass surrounded by water. Earth has seven continents.

country A nation with its own distinct name, land area, government, language, and culture.

crop Vegetables, grains, cotton, or other plants grown by farmers.

culture Customs, traditions, and a way of life that people share.

D

desert An area of hot or cold land that is dry, with little or no rainfall.

E

economy The organization and management of a country's resources, industries, and services.

elevation The height of land above sea level, measured in feet or meters.

environment The natural conditions of an area that include climate, land, and resources.

equator The imaginary line of 0° latitude that circles Earth at its center.

ethnic group People who share traits, such as language, culture, heritage, and lifestyle.

export To send or sell goods to other countries.

F

fertile Land with rich soil that is suitable for growing crops.

fjord A deep, narrow inlet of the sea bordered by steep cliffs; usually created by a glacier.

G

glacier A huge mass of slow-moving ice.

gulf A large bay; an area of a sea or ocean partly enclosed by land.

H

hemisphere A half of Earth that is divided East and West or North and South.

hydroelectric power The use of falling water to produce energy in the form of electricity.

I

iceberg A large, floating ice block that has broken off of a glacier or ice sheet.

import To bring goods in from a foreign country to use or sell.

L

latitude Imaginary horizontal lines measuring distance in degrees north or south of the equator.

longitude Imaginary vertical lines measuring distance in degrees east or west of the prime meridian.

M

mineral Naturally occurring substances within the earth, such as coal, copper, or iron ore.

N

nomads People who move from place to place in search of food, water, and pastures for themselves and animal herds.

O

ocean A huge body of salt water. Oceans cover nearly two-thirds of Earth's surface.

P

peninsula A narrow area of land surrounded on three sides by water.

permafrost Ground that is permanently frozen.

plain An area of land that is low and flat.

population The total number of people living in a region.

prime meridian The imaginary vertical line of 0° that runs through Greenwich, England from the North Pole to the South Pole.

R

rain forest Dense, tropical forest with abundant rainfall and humidity.

resources Substances occuring naturally that have value, such as water and minerals.

rural Having to do with the countryside; opposite of urban.

S

savanna A tree-scattered grassland.

scale The measure of distance on a map as it compares to actual distance.

subsistence farming Farming that produces enough food for farmers, their families, and perhaps a local market, but not enough to sell commercially.

swamp A wetland, or marsh.

T

temperate A mild climate that is neither hot nor cold.

trade The buying, selling, and exchanging of goods within or between countries.

tundra The cold, frozen plains of the Arctic regions.

U

urban Having to do with cities; opposite of rural.

V

volcano An opening in Earth's crust through which lava, steam, and ash erupt.

Index of Major Places on the Maps